To my very de[ar]
"auntie" Joan
With all my love
Michael '10

MANOLO.
A Child in the Spanish Civil War

MANOLO.
A Child in the Spanish Civil War

Miguel Montero

Copyright 2010 Miguel Montero

ISBN 978-1-4461-4641-5

Contents

Prologue ix
Historic Note xi
The Larrumbe School 1
Mass at the Augustines 5
The Shooting Begins 9
Brother Ruperto 15
Facets of Life 21
Fear 25
Ali Baba's Cave 29
Enrique's Execution 33
Slaughter 35
Death Threats 39
Lentils and Potted Cat 43
Sicknesses 51
The Raven 53
The Raven's Pistol 57
El Responsable 63
The Explosion 67
Uncle Jesus's Wounds 73
The Catapult 77
Mystery and Cod Liver Oil 83
At Death's Door 87

The Dead Man	91
Uncle Pepe	95
Aladdin's Lamp	99
The Committee	103
Maximo	107
Guernica	113
Memories	115
Pacho's Death	119
Malaga Wine and Mojicones	123
The Art of Queing	127
The Radio	133
The Doll's House	137
La Carcel Modelo	143
Typhus and Smallpox	147
The Bullet Hole	153
Jail and Scabies	157
Tio Morales	161
Arsenic	167
Boils Galore	175
Pepe's Madness	179
El Brasero	183
Pepe's Journey	187
Stages of Tragedy	191
The White Wolf	195
Adversity	199

The Last Farewell	203
Septicaemia	205
Bullets of Death	209
Desolation	213
Sadness	217
Death	221
One Last Week	223
The Bitter End	227

Prologue

What you are about to read is what I remember from my childhood set against the backcloth of the Spanish Civil War. I was slightly over seven years old at the time. I would have preferred to set my childhood on a pallet of beautiful colours, but as a mere mortal I could not choose where to be then. Destiny did that for me.

This book is neither political nor religious. I am neither. It is simply a recollection of things I saw, heard, and felt. It may sound paradoxical, but because of this, my feelings have always been numb. Whether this is due to my psychological makeup or to the fact that I went through adversity at a very young age, I know not.

I accept life as it is, the everyday merry-go-round of sweetness and bitterness. Circumstances taught me to expect the unexpected and forged the need for survival at all costs, although in my darker moments I wonder if that need should even be considered.

The events I relate happened mainly in Madrid, where I was born. Where my brothers and sisters were born. Where my parents worked hard for a more rewarding living. Madrid, where during three years of agony and hope, the revolution changed my life forever.

Historic Note

Spain suffered the agony of a civil war that started in 1936 and ended in 1939. According to the history books, the right-wing Nationals sought to overthrow Spain's left-wing Republican government, referred to as the Reds.

The Larrumbe School

A wood pigeon landed on the windowsill outside my study. Unexpectedly finding it there gave me a fright. It was young, and its white collar was not showing yet. Rather than the strong plumage that would develop later, light grey down covered its top half. Its tail was already long and strong, and its beak was quite large for a young flier. It stood still, turning its head to watch me as if it knew me from old worried me, and transported me to my childhood.

I was seven when the Spanish Civil War was raging, and in spite of the bullets whizzing past, often too close for comfort, life went on. And so did we.

Those were the days of the Larrumbe School, where Doña Amalia, well upholstered and wearing wire-frame spectacles with round lenses, imparted knowledge to us.

The Larrumbe School was situated on the second floor of a block of ten, where my friend Juanito lived with his two sisters, mom, and dad. At that time, families were important. Parents and children, sons and daughters, were a unit. Couples married and stayed married till death came. There was discipline and harmony. What a contrast with the world of today, where anything goes and wrongdoing is considered just a matter of opinion.

The rectangular classroom housed a plinth for Doña Amalia's desk and chair, plus a number of long green desks and benches large enough for four of us. The desks, more than desks, were flat tables, with holes for our inkwells and an indentation where to place a pen. There were no ballpoint pens, just a metal nib and holder.

Of course, before graduating to the wonders of ink and paper we were taught to write on a slate with a slate pencil. It took me a long time to come to terms with the wisdom of replacing the slate with pencil and paper. In my view, it ruined the business of writing and communicating safely with my peers. When Doña Amalia concentrated on polishing her glasses with such zest that our mischievous activities were not detected, I could display my intellect by drawing her on the slate with an enormous nose and elephant ears, or by writing everybody's favourite naughty words, such as *mierda* or *idiota,* which had a fascinating sound and very little meaning, in safety; at the slightest glimpse of suspicion in her eyes, I quickly erased the clandestine stuff with a swift swipe.

I sat between Juanito and Carlota, who lived in an upstairs flat in the same block as myself. Carlota's father was a policeman and because of that had access to precious goodies like chocolate, which came in packets of ten square ounces. Carlota claimed to have a sack full of it for her own consumption and mine, and during the hard times of the war she shared the chocolate with me – a square ounce of dark brown heaven imprinted with the face of a child drinking the delicious stuff from a round bowl.

Out of school we used to meet on the stairs where she patiently waited for me. Together we would climb to our hiding cocoon on the top floor, a cosy cabbie hole next to the flat roof where a retired Colonel known by the name of Don Cesar, kept hundreds of pigeons.

The transition of slate writing on to paper was eventually mastered by most of us, under a certain disillusion at first. But we did it. Not so El Militino who sat at the far end of our table and was in the habit of silently farting midmorning, as if attached to some miasmatic ritual without which his life would run the risk of extinction. Silent farts were the real McCoy in the release of methane in its most lethal variety. The pong was so intense that Doña Amalia was ready and waiting to open the window as soon as she saw El Militino stirring on his seat with the characteristic motion that accompanied the ritual.

In spite of the horrid smell, we did not object to his effusions, which created a chain reaction of giggles in the classroom. Juanito, Carlota, and myself, being in direct line of fire had a council of war, not so much to try and stop him from expelling the noxious gases, but to find out the cause of it. Juanito, whose clarity of mind was always on display, conducted a tripartite enquiry.

'His dad works in the vegetable shop, doesn't he?'
'He does,' Carlota and I, as usual, agreed.
'And he sells cabbages, doesn't he?'
More agreement.
'El Militino must eat a lot of cabbages.'
'His dad also sells garlics,' I ventured.
'Yuk. Squashed garlic and cabbages. Yuk. Yuk. Yuk.' Carlota emphasised her words with a gesture reserved for special occasions.

'My granddad eats that, and my mum says one day he's going to gas the whole family.'

One day Juanito came to school with a glint in his eye. I sensed he was planning something. 'I'm going to outfart El Militino,' he told me in a whisper, twisting his mouth. Mission impossible. Brave decision! I passed the message to Carlota and waited.

Midmorning came and as expected, El Militino performed. Doña Amalia opened the window. Seconds later Juanito let one off with sonorous sound effects. Juanito has obviously gone beyond his capabilities. The miasma from his entrails did not disperse as it did with El Militino's silent specimens. Juanito gave me a miserable look, which told me he had surpassed his own expectations. A great achievement at a high price. Doña Amalia, a real eagle at spotting trouble, called for reinforcements in the person of her daughter, Mari Paz, who escorted him, red faced and eyes cast down, to his home, only a few flights of stairs away, for a change of pants.

Mass at the Augustines

My days at the Larrumbe School started before the war did. Early in the morning of July 18th, 1936 all hell broke loose. I was then a few months into my seventh year, and as such, I witnessed events in a different light than I would do now.

We lived, like everybody else, in a flat; with the exception of a few residential zones, there were no houses in Madrid, just blocks of flats raising generally six to eight floors. At street level, there was a variety of shops: butcher, baker, fishmonger, greengrocer, general food store, even a coal merchant and a *taverna* on the corner of the street right opposite the milk shop.

At the far end of the street stood the Augustines church where we went to mass every Sunday morning. It was a Latin affair that nobody understood, but the congregation stood and listened attentively – the lucky ones sat and listened attentively, too.

The church was always packed to the extent that latecomers had to fight their way in through a solid mass of humanity and remain by the swinging door, often buffeted by it when even-later comers tried to gain entry. It was essential to get in before the Gospel for the mass to be valid. Failing that, a mortal sin would stain the soul, only to be cleansed by confession, repentance, and summary punishment or penance imposed by the father confessor according to his benign or severe mood.

I was not of an age to qualify for confession and neither was Juanito. His mind being of a scientific nature, he could not wait for the day we would go to confession so that we could compare notes.

Although the Augustines was rather spacious, the fervour of the Catholic flock could have benefited from a much larger place of worship.

Every Sunday before the war, everybody went to mass in their best behaviour and clothes.

I walked to the church in the company of my sister Maria four years older than me and our friend Carmina who lived in our block and was also older. None of us knew exactly how to respond to the priest's ritual. So to be on the safe side my mother told us to do what any of the older ladies did. We settled for that and chose as our guide a gaunt woman dressed in black, head covered with a veil of the same mournful colour. A distinct uniform worn in readiness for the gates of heaven. We were not disappointed with our choice, as she seemed to be more active than the others. We genuflected with her, did the sign of the cross with her, answered the priest in our best Latin the extent of which was a kind of muffled sing- song that we executed with outmost seriousness. We felt good being able to follow the mass like the rest of the worshipers. Half way through the ceremony our guide introduced new material into the rituals that we proudly followed as we were sure she possessed the exclusive rights. It consisted in making the sign of the cross over her mouth every so often. So we stuck with it until a mildly irate old fellow bent down to Maria and said sternly:

'You should know better than making fun of the old lady.'

Not understanding the meaning of that, Maria could not fathom out the severity of the reprimand. I got a clip around the ear for my share of guilt. Carmina, luckily ducked in time to avoid his wrath. I would not have liked it if he had hit her.

When we returned home my mother explained:

'The old lady was probably yawning'. An explanation that went down a treat on my list of things not to do in church unless boredom compelled me to do so.

After mass Carmina would take me by the hand to Sennor Aragon pharmacy only a few minutes walk away to buy a liquorice bar each and a few aniseed twists that we shared. With the goodies we sat on the kerb outside our block to indulge in the black tarry juice of the liquorice. Some of the aniseed twists I reserved for night time in bed.

Carmina was nine what I considered being a real big girl. She took great care of me. Always had a hanky ready to wipe off any dribble that accidentally ran out of my mouth.

The church constituted an integral part of family life. The word community was not known as it is now when nobody knows what it really means.

Beside masses, which were always celebrated in the morning, the Augustines provided a nine evening supplement called 'la novena', the main ingredients of which were the rosary and the litany, mainly attended by women including my mother. With a lesser attendance than to mass there was enough room for sitting. My mother liked to sit on the front pew to have a better view of the altar below a presiding Jesus Christ attired in a bloody loincloth and crown of thorns. A scene I did not care much for, as I could not understand, not then, not now, how a crucified man could be any use to save our souls. I am sure a less drastic way could be found. With the exception of that unpleasant sight, I also liked sitting there and entertained myself gazing at the flickering of the candles and filling my nose with the smell of wax. But my preferred smell was that of rosemary, plentiful around the church. Combined with the whiffs of incense, it compelled me to daydream in order to escape the boredom of too many Hail Marys and Gloria Patris.

The droning of the litany, with its almost toneless whispering, induced sleep difficult to resist. The all-Latin litany was viewed as *conditio sine qua non* the novena could exist. Even now, so many years away from my childhood, many of the lines still ring in my ears. It took me a while to discover the meaning of the phrases I had listened to and repeated many times. To my joy, I discovered that *sursumcordam* actually means 'lift up your hearts'. *Turris eburnean* translates as 'ivory tower', and I gather it was intended as a compliment to the Virgin Mary. I wonder if a woman of today would consider that a compliment, whether she would find it 'sexy' enough to appreciate it.

La novena was not always a boring affair. Sometimes my friend Juanito would come with us, and after sitting on the pew awhile, we would disappear beyond a side of the altar steps to play the equivalent of shove halfpenny. On occasion, Brother Ruperto, a venerable ancient man who was loved by everybody, would join us his eyes glinting with joy.

There was something about Brother Ruperto that invited people to confide in him. Later, when I was older, I learnt that he gave the grown-ups guidance for their problems. He was a kind of early councillor whose aim was to smooth the jagged edges of life.

He ran the church choir where two of my brothers and my sister Maria sang. My family had a warm affection for him, especially my mother. She was ever grateful for his help in taking some of her kids from under her feet during those singing sessions.

The Shooting Begins

Sometime in the morning of July 18th, we had the first frightening taste of the war. The sun was shining at its brightest, as it always did in the summer in Madrid, which was notorious for being encumbered by six months of winter and six months of hell. Spring and autumn were too ephemeral to be considered seasons. The summers, then, were dry and implacably hot. The temperature was so high that all public transport came to a halt between the hours of one and three in the afternoon.

With the exception of some cobbled streets, most of them were asphalted. It was not unusual to see my footprints following me when I crossed the street – the heat was capable of softening the asphalt to almost melting point. The summer sky, permanently blue and cloudless, became a boring sight.

Madrid, the capital of Spain, is situated in the centremost point of the Iberian Peninsula, as far away from the sea as can be. It is surrounded by mountains that prevent the thermostatic effect from the sea. Aided and abetted by a high population density, the capital turns into a gigantic slow cooker in the summer. The night gives no relief from the heat because of the absence of wind.

We lived in Barrio de Salamanca, a prime residential quarter. Our street Calle del General Oraa terminated in La Castellana, a main avenue of the Capital. The boulevards were planted with a profusion of trees, a much-welcomed umbrella to shade us from the rays of the sun.

Winters can be described as the exact opposite, with cutting winds and very low temperatures.

Somebody told Juanito once that on extremely cold days, his pee would freeze before reaching the ground. So, his mind always ready for the challenge of the unknown, he devised a method to produce iced pee. It was decided that he, El Militino, as strong at pissing as he was at farting, and myself would pee in an empty can of pilchards in tomato sauce that we took to a field nearby. The three of us got ready. Willies between our fingers and at the command of *mear*! (pee) we let our urine flow squeezing the end of our willies to give it pressure. If Juanito's inventiveness had been successful, we would have been the first trio in history to produce iced piss in cylindrical form. Instead, we got our willies almost frostbitten.

That was a winter game.

But that day in July, the heat was intense and the warm smell of the acacias filled the air. I was watching Maria painting with watercolours when strange noises came from outside. Our flat had ten open balconies facing the street. Being situated on the second floor, known as the principal, it was easy to see the out-of-doors activities, not only across the street but also along a sizable part of its length. The Augustines Church was an austere structure two or three hundred meters away from our block, on the same side of the street.

As the unfamiliar noise kept on repeating itself, Maria and I looked through the ajar balcony doors and saw a group of men with shotguns and rifles. The men were not in uniform. Suddenly my mother ran from the kitchen into the dining room, where we were. 'Come away from that balcony,' she told us.

'What's that noise, Mum?'

'Shotgun... shotgun fire.' She said this as casually as she could, not wanting to alarm us, but as the shots persisted her calm was eroded. She put her arms around us and hurriedly took us to the entrance hall, a secluded place away from the balconies. There, we knelt down and prayed.

'Those men are shooting at the church. God help us!'

The rifles were rattling a scary song.

We stayed put, not quite understanding what was happening. Little did we know that tragedy that would affect the whole country was brewing. My mother was right. We were going to need the help of God and all his celestial court for good measure.

The prerogative of childhood is that children can go from tears to laughter, from fright to courage quickly. For this reason, our scary moment soon dissolved and some kind of comical valour took over.

The flat was designed like a train carriage with a long corridor into which the doors of the different rooms opened. All had spacious balconies, including the kitchen. The toilet was next to it, at the far end of the corridor with the entrance hall at the other. The hall was the only part of the flat in the dark. It was a relatively peaceful place, where my mother and our cat found refuge on stormy days. There, the lightning was not seen and the sound of thunder became somewhat muted. Now that the war was, so far, on the outside, we all gathered there when it massacred the peace of the neighbourhood.

The first pang of fright over, Maria and I would march up and down the corridor, helmeted with colanders, imitating the men in the street below with a broomstick, which we shared in turns, poised like a rifle. Muffled sound effects added drama to the fun.

It did not take us long to differentiate between the sound of a rifle firing and the flat thudding of the bullets embedding themselves in the church's wall.

Our daredevil spirit soon grew stronger, and instead of limiting ourselves to marching along the corridor, we made frequent incursions into the rooms, mimicking the armed men. Most of them were belly down on the pavement as if expecting saintly Brother Ruperto to attack them with some divine weapon in the shape of a hand grenade.

My father, talking to my mother and assuming we were out of earshot, said, 'Quite ridiculous. These are ignorant *jobos* recruited by the Reds.'

It did not make much sense to me but automatically gave me the green light to surreptitiously widen the gap in the balcony doors and shoot at them with my makeshift rifle, which caused my mother to have a nervous reaction that bordered on apoplexy.

Our cat, a female with the masculine name of Michito, had been with the family since before I was born. All black and round faced, he had a highly developed sense of diplomatic behaviour, avoiding my eldest brother's shoe when he was about, accompanying my mother to the hall when thunder was loose in the sky or bullets rained in every direction. He had a remarkable sense of humanity. When I was ill, he would sit outside my bedroom door. It was only when I was better that he would come in and lie at the foot of my bed. When there was no other activity, he would do the rounds of the rooms, looking for a comfortable place to have one of his many naps.

Another family member was La Chugue, a tortoise who hibernated in a corner of the kitchen. La Chugue was a working family member in charge of pest control. Her speciality was cockroaches of all colours and sizes. She caught brown ones with slender bodies and high-speed legs by swiftly darting her little head out of the shell with incredible speed for such a slow-moving animal. Those she missed perished under my foot. Another variety was the king-size cockroach with a shiny black body, as if it was made of jet. A real treat! I can still hear the squashing sound when they were crushed in La Chugues powerful beak-like mandibles, which were left dripping with a gooey, viscous residue. I avoided executing those; I would have to remove the mess left on the quarry tiles that covered the floor, for fear of being chastised.

The main source of cockroaches, I was told, was in the coal stored under the kitchen range, our only source of heating for cooking and boiling water and milk. In those days, there was no central heating, no hot water, no bathroom, no washbasin. Ablutions, normally restricted to the face, were performed in the kitchen sink, a large stone affair, where La Chugue swam as a treat for services rendered.

We washed with cold water and a cubic chunk of soap, amber in colour, displaying a lizard on its topside. *Jabon Lagarto* (Lizard Soap).

Whole-body immersion was not possible, so from time to time, we suffered partial washes. I washed, or rather, de-scaled my feet in a zinc bowl once a week – or less often if I could get away with it. Soap alone was not enough to remove the crust accumulated over many days of avoiding contact with water. A bundle of esparto grass was also used for washing up.

The kitchen was a fairly spacious place that had multiple uses. In winter, it was my favourite place for warmth whenever the range was on. It was also the place where my mother displayed her medical skills. Maria and I referred to it as the *lavativa* (enema) room, as on those occasions when our bellies were banged up, an enema of warm water and a smear of olive oil around the arsehole did the job with incredible efficiency. For this sophisticated treatment, I sat on my father's wooden toolbox and watched my mother prepare the enema dispenser, a pear-shaped rubber instrument that she handled with the dexterity of experience. When things were ready, I would bend over said wooden toolbox and wait for the warm water to flow through my back passage. To say that the effect was not instantaneous would be a travesty of the truth, so not wasting any time, I transferred my bum onto an ad hoc chamber pot. The whole performance took place with the balcony doors fully open to mitigate the aroma.

The business at hand finished, my mother used to exclaim, 'Gloria bendita' (blessed glory), which I thought were appropriate words to define a state of blissful satisfaction.

Many things were multipurpose, and so were the enema dispensers. It was a wonderful weapon to shower cockroaches with water and to fight between ourselves when there were no adults about.

At Christmas, before the war, a capon or two established their quarters in a corner of the kitchen to spend their final days. We became fond of them, christened them with exotic names, fed them out of our hands, and together with Michito, at his best behaviour, enjoyed their company. On the eve of the festivities, one of my older brothers would take them to Pepita, the embroiderer, who lived in an upstairs flat, and with great dexterity, Pepita slit their combs. After a short dance with bright red blood pouring from their heads, they slumped onto the floor, soon to be returned to our kitchen. Although we did not have the heart or the skill to put the capons to sleep, we did not have any romantic feelings about their departure, which we saw as part of the celebrations. I watched Pepita skilfully brandish the knife and saw the capons die in front of my feet. I accepted the episode without any feeling of sadness or remorse. The capons were for us to eat. And that was that. Pepita was paid in kind with some of the giblets and feet.

I was given the task to help one of my brothers or sisters – I had four of each – to defeather the birds. We all participated in this activity. When everything was ready, my mother would do the cooking and all of us, the eating.

Brother Ruperto

The shooting continued. Shouts and threats mingled with the shattering of glass. The Gothic arched windows of the church were a new target. At one point, the firing ceased and Brother Ruperto appeared through a side entrance. Calmly, he crossed the street to meet the group of men, who looked doubtful of what to do and stood in confusion. Amongst them was Roberto, the deliveryman from the groceries shop and, so far, an assiduous churchgoer.

Brother Ruperto spoke: 'Leave your weapons and come to the church with me.'

'We're not leaving our arms.'

'Then bring them with you, but come with me.'

The men followed like protesting children.

I remember Brother Ruperto as a corpulent man who could have shaken any of them by the scruff of the neck in spite of his advanced years. His basso profundo voice always commanded quiet authority.

By the church door, they stopped. There was some disagreement as to whether to follow the saintly brother inside or not.

'Religion is the opium of the people,' uttered one of them, stumbling over the words.

'God does not fucking exist,' ventured a visibly angry man much older than the rest.

'Los curas son todos unos hijos de puta' (priests are the sons of whores).

'Down with the church.'

'And the nuns.'

'Kill them all.'

'Fuck them first.'

Coarse laughter exploded.

'Please don't let anger make you say those things.' Brother Ruperto was unperturbed. The men shuffled about, looking at one another as if expecting one of them to take charge.

'How many nuns have you shagged on the quiet? You bloody old git.'

Anger was turning into menacing violence in the deserted street. Windows closed. Behind them, people were too scared to intervene. The news that Madrid was in the hands of the Reds had soon travelled.

'If you want us to follow you into the church, we will, but it is not to say the Our Father.'

'It will be to spit on the paten.'

'And drink your wine in the bleeding chalice.'

'And when we've done we'll burn the crappy place.'

'We'll stamp on the crucifix till we smash it to pieces.'

'And all the statues of the virgin.'

'She was no virgin. Saint Joseph tore her "seal of guarantee" with his fucking cock.'

There was a silence, a golden opportunity for coughing and spitting, but the men were still utterly disorganised and undecided as to how to proceed.

Brother Ruperto listened to this barrage of blasphemy silently. Only his hands and body language refuted what was being said. Grabbing a brief pause when the vociferous men seemed to be preparing for another verbal onslaught, he took Roberto by the arm and said, 'Roberto, this is not like you. I've known you since you were a baby. I christened you. You come to mass on Sundays. You know how we help people in need. You know the life of sacrifice the nuns endure.' His voice did not falter; instead, it seemed to become Roberto's conscience talking, causing him to glue his eyes on the ground. He did not dare to look at Brother Ruperto.

'Death to the old bastard.'

'Don't let him talk himself out of dying.'

Roberto freed himself and pushed Brother Ruperto away.

A man punched Brother Ruperto in the stomach, booted feet kicked him, and in spite of that, he managed to stay up. Roberto, as if contaminated by some contagious fever slapped him on the face.

'Not you, Roberto, not you.'

The words stopped. The victim was dragged into the church. After that, an agonising silence fell in the street. Out of sight, we heard a terrible commotion: The screams, as if from animals on the rampage. The stamping of booted feet. The crash of objects falling to the floor. And amongst that melange of madness that could only belong to rabid dogs, we heard the dominating voice of Brother Ruperto start a prayer that he would never finish.

Nobody saw what happened in the Agustines the rest of the day or during the night. But when morning came, the body of Brother Ruperto was found transfixed to a tree in Principe de Vergara's boulevard adjacent to the church, with a bayonet through the stomach. His abdomen was cut open, his cassock at his feet, and his intestines exposed in a bloody gooey mess. His face was unrecognisable.

I saw and heard this through my uncle Jesus's eyes and words. He lived opposite the Augustines, in a prime position to witness the horrific events.

There is only so much adults can keep from the knowledge of children, and by intuition or the heightened awareness I developed during those bitter days, I fathomed out the gravity of the situation. An era of terror was dawning in Spain. Most of the country was in the hands of the Reds, bastard offsprings of Russian communism that adopted *The International* as their hymn and splashed the hammer and sickle on a red flag.

The revolution had started. The wind of change was blowing like a hurricane, albeit in the wrong direction. The promoters of the new era tried to impose on the country ideas that were abhorrent to the Spanish people. They made the greatest mistake in attacking the church. To anybody whose intelligence was not comparable to that of a banana skin, this was obviously a non-starter. If those who had set up this venture had only listened to Don Quixote as he explained the power of the Church to Sancho Panza: *'Sancho, con la Iglesia hemos topado'* (you'll never win a battle against the Church), the Reds might, just might, have had a chance for victory. But instead of that, they kicked off the revolution by murdering thirteen bishops and some six thousand nuns and priests. That was only the beginning of the carnage.

In the evening, Uncle Jesus came to see my father. He looked ashen. The large mustachios that rode his upper lip quivered when he spoke. He did not pick me up and play as he usually did when he visited; instead, he went straight into the dining room, where my father was reading *The ABC,* our daily paper.

Maria and I were sent to Carmina's flat, a few flights of stairs up. There was nothing unusual in this; we often got together there to play ludo. But that evening, there was some urgency in sending us out of the house. On our way out, Uncle Pedro and Uncle Fabian also came to see my father. We thought this strange because the four of them worked together.

My father and my three uncles owned a garage and workshop, which was only a block and a half from our flat. That must have been a rarity at the time, almost seventy years ago, when cars were the domain of the very rich. Machinery capable of turning metal into spare parts and an array of other items such as tools have become commonplace through the years.

I loved to go and see my father in his office sitting at his desk, a dark wood piece of furniture, partly covered with burgundy leather. On the centre of the desk were two inkwells, one filled with red ink, the other with blue-black. A silver tray contained several pens and pencils. A banker's lamp in gold with a green shade to shelter the eyes from the light presided over the desk. On a corner of the office, as if in quarantine before possible use, was an Underwood typewriter in black. Like a harbinger of the future, hiding in the shadows, it projected the power of the unknown and whetted my appetite to get my fingers on to the round keys.

I cannot remember if there was a telephone in his office, although I assume there must have been one. In my memory, I see a wall-mounted one outside. I can still see the number 53208 in bold digits on the centre dial.

Those were the days when telephones in Madrid could only be used for local calls, which were free. Long-distance calls posed difficulties, and people had to go to one of the Telefonica (telephone company) offices where there was always a queue. The call had to be booked. Then there was an indeterminate wait for an available line and, to crown it all, the lack of privacy, as the operators, all female, were notorious for listening in.

With no fax, Internet, or email and the difficulty and expense of the telephone, telegrams were another source of communication. Because of the cost, brevity was of the essence and telegrams were mainly used to convey important news such as: 'Mum critical' stop; 'Auntie Dolores in hospital' stop; 'Send money' stop; or a frivolous one: 'Conchita married at last', stop.

My father dealt mainly with the running of the business, while Uncle Pedro, whose office was next door, separated by a glass partition, devoted himself to the administration. Unlike my other two uncles, he was a stern individual who hardly smiled. As the oldest, he considered it a duty to exercise his authority over the others. This may sound strange today but all those years ago, it was an accepted norm.

The smell of petrol and grease still lingers in my memory, and so do the multitude of noises I heard in the workshop: the metallic chattering of the machinery, the resounding clapping of the presses, the hissing of the air lines inflating tyres. But above all, it is petrol, with its heady scent that penetrates the senses, that made a mark in my memory. This scent is now not as I remember it. Lots of things have changed, and so has the scent of my childhood.

Uncle Jesus and Uncle Fabian worked on the machines. One was a turner and the other a vertical lathe operator. My older brothers and cousins followed suit later. There were few non-family operatives. 'It is important to get to know the business from scratch to be successful.' This was a maxim repeated by Uncle Pedro ad infinitum.

The garage and workshop were enormous. As I recall, there was always great activity in the workshop, where three or four men in dark blue overalls, a real grease patrol, attended to vehicle repairs. In contrast, the garage was a deserted place, and with the exception of the odd chauffer coming to take a car away for a few moments of freedom, the only regulars to be seen there were Julian and Silvester, general dog's bodies known as Los Mozos. I got on famously with them, as they always had time to entertain me. Later, when the war progressed, I learned that one of them was a dark horse and not to be trusted. For a time, nobody knew which one was the enemy within.

The garage was flanked on either side of its entire length by self-contained parking bays with scissor doors. The functioned more as living accommodations, where a car spent most of its life, than as parking bays. One in particular occupied the bay adjacent to the entrance and languished there on chocks, an immobile fixture. Its owner, according to Uncle Fabian, was an ambassador to some South American country.

Next to it was our own car, a Mercedes-Benz known among the family as El Benz. More than a saloon, it could now be compared to a medium-size passenger and general-purpose vehicle, with a collapsible grey canopy and bench seats on either side of the seating area. It had a hand brake outside the driver's cab and a spare wheel on the outside.

Before the war, El Benz took my father, uncles, older brothers, and cousins hunting to Boadilla del Monte, some twenty kilometres from Madrid, where hares and pheasants abounded. On their return, the smell of the game – that of the leather pouches and the lingering evidence left by gunpowder trapped in the barrels of the shotguns – invaded the flat.

Some Sundays in the summer, when the heat was at its most intense, El Benz would fill up with the younger kids of yesterday, the wrinklies of today, and delivered us to the river, where we splashed about and our skins were burnt red like boiled lobsters.

El Benz was a much-loved family symbol. Its rhythmic moaning rocked me to sleep many times as it drove along. Many photographs were taken showing its majestic beauty. And many more were taken with its canopy down and with the whole family loaded on board. El Benz was our mascot.

Facets of Life

Doña Carmen, Carmina's mother, greeted us with a bowl of hot chocolate and *rosquillas,* a kind of circular cookie partly covered with icing sugar and flavoured with aniseed, to set the right mood for the ludo games.

Carlota, who invariably sat on the corner next to mine in order to kick me under the table when she wanted me to move a counter to her advantage, had been helping to make the hot chocolate out of her supply from the famous sack her father acquired exclusively for her.

'Now, children, we shall all go to the dining room and have this lovely chocolate that Carlota has made,' said Doña Carmen, adding a lot of praise for Carlota's culinary talent. This was necessary to keep Carlota, who possessed a mischievous streak that often got her into hot water, in an obedient mood. Any upsetting of the ludo board, either by accident or on purpose when she was losing, had to be pre-empted.

Carlota smiled – a promise of good behaviour! It was a brown smile with chocolate-coated lips that matched a few stains of the same nature on her apron.

The dining room was pentagonal with a glass covered *mirador,* a kind of enclosed large balcony, which provided a wonderful observation point, due to the position of the block; built on the crossing of two streets it resembled a kind of crucible.

It was fun to watch women getting in and out of the shops, some stopping for a chin wag on their way; people just going about their business; children playing on the pavement; or the ice-delivery van unloading huge bars that were left outside the taverna until Vitor, the wine man, appeared with a long hook to slide them in. On occasions the knife-grinder would set up his contraption and shout an invitation to have knives and scissors sharpened, an operation that called for my concentrated attention. If I could only get those sparks out of the blades like he did simply by making the wheel turn with his foot,

I would be the envy of my friends, especially Juanito, who always wanted to impress the rest of us with his bright ideas.

On other occasions we were visited by the umbrella repairer, whose skills extended to metal pots of all kinds. He was a gipsy, accompanied by two or three of his children, whose job it was to collect broken umbrellas, pots, and pans, including frying pans, to be repaired. Those were the days when repairs were an alternative to replacing things with new ones. Perhaps cooking utensils were of an inferior quality to those of today, or perhaps they were put to a harder life, having to contend with the kitchen range rather than a gas or an electric cooker. Umbrellas were secondary; they were not used much, due to the scarcity of rain.

The honey vendor, who came all the way from La Alcarria, professed to bring 'the best honey in the world'. He kept the golden stuff in earthenware pots from which he transferred it into the buyer's container.

But that evening while we dunked the rosquillas in the hot chocolate and watched the street below, the familiar scene of shoppers, those offering a variety of goods and services, and casual passers-by had changed. A forever thriving, busy neighbourhood had become an almost deserted place where a few *milicianos* (soldiers of the revolution), some in uniform, some not, could be seen patrolling the street in a haphazard way. Civilians seldom stopped to talk to them, with the exception of some men who were strange to the neighbourhood. Later, not much later, others would join these milicianos, men with beards and rough uniforms, properly armed and high booted, who spoke languages we did not understand – and sometimes even they found it difficult to communicate amongst themselves. Those were mainly mercenaries from the International Brigades, paid soldiers who fought for money and killed the citizens of a country in turmoil. The International Brigades and a bunch of misguided idealists did not take long to stick their noses where they were not wanted.

A Pilot radio was on, volume reduced to a low whisper broadcasting something I could not understand. With its conical dome and lattice grill sporting a yellowish illuminated little window where the station frequencies showed, it fascinated me, To me, it sounded like the garbled chatter of a man with a deep voice. But that garbled chatter must have meant something to Doña Carmen, whose face became sombre as the broadcast went on. Maria seemed to understand what the man with the deep voice was saying and sometime after gave me her own version of what was happening.

All in all, we had a good time. Carlota was at her best behaviour, my sister played the role of grown-up to perfection, and Carmina – always watching after me – wiped my mouth every time a drop of chocolate threatened to spoil my clean shirt.

When we came down, the dinner table, a large circular specimen of oak, was already set. Soon the eleven of us sat round it, Maria and I on either side of my father, my mother and two older sisters by the door to enable them to bring the food from the kitchen, and the rest in their respective places.

My father acted as if nothing new was taking place, but when he hugged me good night after dinner, I felt something hard and bulky under his jacket. Maria also felt the same thing, but she would not tell me what it was.

Fear

As the days went by, the situation at home became more unsettled. Maria and I, being 'the children', were told never to answer the door. My mother and the more grown brothers and sisters were told never to allow a stranger to come in. The heavy wooden door was fitted with a *mirilla,* an opening with a grill on the outside and a metal shutter on the inside, as on a speakeasy door. The mirilla allowed the family to scrutinize the caller. Maria and I were not tall enough to reach it.

In the evenings, when my father was home he took that task upon himself, always carrying the hard, bulky thing in his pocket. Maria explained the precautions. Father had been sent anonymous threats on his life. The atmosphere of unease spread like an unwanted smell, affecting mainly my mother, who had the unenviable job of looking after all of us. I do not remember feeling scared. I just felt curious about the unusual goings-on.

Details that might have been considered trivial could now mean the difference between life and death. Possessing something that the revolutionaries considered a sign against the new ideas should be well hidden or, better still, destroyed to remain safe.

The colours of the Spanish flag, gold, red, and gold, were changed to red, gold, and purple by the Republic. Anybody in possession of the original flag could be severely punished. The same applied to images of Christ, the Virgin Mary, sacred hearts, crucifixes, and the like. I never had any time for this exhibition of ugliness and never understood why people were hell-bent on clogging up wall space with images in fading brown, sepia, and black, an undisputable triumvirate of colours to depress the most cheerful of mortals.

Christ crucified, as I saw it in church, made me think of all those who were sentenced to death by crucifixion and what horrendous suffering it must have been for them. The underlying effect of all these icons left me in a void of confusion. However, that was the very character of the Spanish people, and trying to take this away from them was utter foolishness.

For the sake of safety, all this clobber had to be got rid of. This was a mammoth task, considering that Spain was a Catholic country of long standing. Words such as God, virgin, saint, glory, religion, and similar concepts were considered obscurantist and had to be erased from books. Whether this was an official directive by the Reds or not, I never found out. But in those days when fear was widespread, the maxim 'prevention better than cure', became the order of the day.

At the Larrumbe school, Doña Amalia instructed us in the discipline of crossing words off books, while wiping tears from her eyes. El Militino soon excelled at this new art form and approached it with great devotion, his tongue sticking out of the corner of his mouth, left cheek almost touching the desk, and crayon travelling to and fro over the 'obscurantist' words. Juanito, always at the helm of innovation, discovered that this task would not be complete without crossing off few more for the sake of beautifying the page with an unusual pattern.

Doña Amalia was visibly subdued, her soul softened to the extent that while chanting the multiplication tables at the end of the day, she did not have the strength to correct El Militino, who was the only boy in class who 'knew' that three times three amounts to twenty-seven. In spite of the grief that overpowered her, I detected a brief spark of anger that I knew would bring revenge the following day.

I remember my mother hiding a number of silk handkerchiefs that had been handed down from her grandmother, decorated with the original flag, and the portrait of Alfonso the XII. She hid them in the entrails of a mattress. Mattresses then were a favourite hiding place for many things, as they were not made with a conglomeration of springs enclosed in a frame and covered with some pretty cloth. Mattresses were more comparable to a thick duvet or a big sack full of wool tufts.

Another thing to hide were a number of silver coins, reserved for 'after the war'. Those were secreted in my mother's and sisters' whalebone corsets. A corset was a real coat of armour, capable, with the reinforcement of silver, of withstanding the impact of the horns of a fighting bull.

Lenin's doctrine that property belongs to the nation and not to private individuals spread like wildfire amongst the proletariat, who hoped to take businesses away from their rightful owners. This was a step towards the downfall of the nation.

The post of *El Responsable* (the responsible one) was created. El Responsible was an overseer with ample power to make sure that business were run according to the new rules. My father and uncles, as owners of both the garage and workshop, were put under the control of El Responsable and their rights and authority taken away.

El Benz was requisitioned for military and civilian purposes. At first it remained in our garage, driven by Silvester as decreed by El Responsable. I often saw it driving past our balconies full of milicianos in green uniforms. Later, when the conflict had gained momentum, El Benz would disappear from our sight for days on end and return covered in muck like I had never seen it before. A sorry state for the family symbol!

Luckily, El Responsable was a fairly young man whose main asset was his zest for the progress of the 'people'. Apart from that, his knowledge of management was still to be developed, so being an intelligent man, he limited his powers to giving the appearance that he had things under control, to satisfy his own bosses. In spite of the fact that they got well together, the imposition of El Responsable meant a cut to the emoluments of my father and uncles and an unavoidable feeling of resentment towards the new regime.

Later, when I was older, Uncle Jesus related to me what went on that evening when my father and my uncles got together in the dining room.

The situation looked grim and they decided to arm themselves. The usurpation of what they had worked hard to achieve was difficult to swallow. They were aggravated by the appointment of El Responsable, an ever-present irritant. At times, catastrophe loomed as a gathering storm. Grievances and accusations sparked disputes between family and non-family personnel. Two sides were formed, one for my father and uncles, the other against them, and this resulted in stropolous behaviour and death threats.

Ali Baba's Cave

Midmorning one Saturday, Carlota was waiting for me, sitting on a triangular wooden bench between the second and third floors. She liked sitting there; it had a good view of our flat door, and the bench was low enough for her feet to touch the floor. There were several similar benches on other landings, to afford a slight recovery for those who lived on the upper floors.

Amongst the habitual users of the bench was Doctor Coronel, a living replica of Oliver Hardy, with the addition of diesel-engine heavy breathing. His brother Antonio was a quantity surveyor, and not such a good example of excellent nourishment. Senor Carrillo was stoned out of his wits every Friday night to compensate for the abstinence of meat. This was imposed by the stifling Catholic Church and enforced by his other half. She was given to brandishing whichever object was close at hand when contradicted, a short fat woman, always dressed as if ready to attend a funeral, with massive chestnut hair that struggled to cover what looked like three hard-boiled eggs that grew out of the top of her head. Recently, I have learned that those eruptions are called sebaceous cysts in the medical circles.

The idea of installing a lift had not occurred to the makers of the block, which was an old construction. The main attraction was the large area of balcony space, which would put to shame the most advanced sanatorium design.

Under normal circumstances, it would have been logical for Carlota to just knock on our door when she wanted to see me. But my mother objected to her presence on the grounds that being friends with a policeman's daughter was as good as consorting with the enemy. This she never openly told me, but Juanito and El Militino seemed to have found the reason.

'Your mum doesn't like her because she farts.' A powerful argument of genuine El Militino brand.

'No. Carlota doesn't fart,' Juanito, who claimed to be her best friend, retorted.

But El Militino pursued his point. 'How do you know? She may be a secret farter.'

Juanito's feelings were hurt. 'She's a girl. Girls don't do that.' He defended her with that final irrefutable statement. Then he added, 'She may be a spy for the Reds. Her dad's a policeman. You've got to be a Red to be a policeman now.' Argument settled.

But as far as I was concerned, with all her tricks and tantrums, she was my friend and my only supplier of chocolate.

When I appeared I saw her, now standing on the bench, waving a book at me. 'It's Tom Thumb. Has pop-up pictures. Let's go read it.' We ran up the stairs as fast as our feet would take us, and into our hiding hole we went.

The top of the building had a terrace where Don Cesar kept his pigeons housed in neatly stacked compartments painted in a blue grey mat finish with black numbers. I was amazed at how the pigeons could find their own addresses. 'It's simple, Manolo,' he explained, 'that is what the numbers are for.' Not that I believed his explanation, but it seemed to be a fair one.

The rear of the terrace was surrounded by a sloping roof of dark red pantiles. Within it, a profusion of chimneypots let the smoke from the kitchen ranges into an ever-blue sky. Whilst exploring, we had discovered a hatch where the roof met the terrace. A narrow gap allowed us in with a bit of a squeeze. We christened the hatch Ali Baba's Cave. The magic words 'Ali Baba' were necessary to gain entrance. Through the gaps in the pantiles, we had a panoramic view of rooftops and shorter buildings and above all, a close-up of the pigeons, which we considered the carriers of our own imaginary messages.

We browsed through the book that she had duly marked with her name, Carlota Gracia, in large round pencil lettering. Then we became engrossed in Tom Thumb's plight as he got lost in the forest, his trail of bits of bread eaten by the birds.

In Juanito's judgement, Tom would have been much better off borrowing a bobbin of cotton from his mum's sewing box. 'All he had to do,' Juanito explained, 'was to tie one end of the thread to the cabin door where they lived and let the thread run free as they walked. Then returning home would be easy, just by winding up the thread.' He suggested we put this bright idea into practice to prove his point.

Engrossed as we were, our attention was diverted from the story when Marina appeared on the terrace, wiping her eyes and leading her partner by the hand. Rumour had it, Marina lived with Don Cesar in an unmarried state, a sin before the eyes of God and the neighbours. They sat on wicker chairs and remained silent for a while.

'His face is bleeding.'

'His mouth is all purple.'

We had never seen Don Cesar looking so squashed; it was quite the opposite of the image we had of him, tall, smiling, and happy-looking. Nor had we seen Marina crying so copiously.

The scene we witnessed was the result of a night raid by the secret police, who manhandled him into a car and took him to a *cheka,* a headquarters cell. I knew through hearing snippets of conversations no one had the slightest hope of coming out of a cheka unscathed. The Reds established them as places where suspects were taken for interrogation, torture, and finally, depuration or death.

The system was worked brutally, hidden under the banner that extreme situations call for extreme solutions. This maxim was reinforced by the belief that the Nationals were also engaged in a ruthless policy. Not many people doubted that the Civil War was a bitter, albeit necessary, fight,.

Men and a negligible number of women were apprehended on the flimsiest suspicion and taken to the dreaded chekas. Even some supporters of the Reds ended up captured in this way. The interrogation was peppered with verbal and physical assault. Accusations, many times false, were shouted at the detainees in an attempt to find out their true colours. A favourite method of encouraging the suspects to speak was to force them to stare at a powerful lamp for as long as the interrogators deemed necessary.

Don Cesar never gave details of his treatment but the look of him after having been worked on in the cheka was clear evidence of what he might have gone through.

It was rumoured that an article had been published in a daily paper under the title 'The Ex-Commandant and His Pigeons'. The article accused him of being a collaborator with the Nationals, when in truth he had served in the Republican Army. A mistake of this kind was not uncommon, but in the climate of terror the country was going through, there was no valid apology by the press.

Carlota and I were marooned in Ali Baba's Cave. We sat silently on our haunches, as still as we could so as not to be discovered. Time passed slowly. Every minute was a reminder that our parents would soon be searching for us.

Don Cesar suddenly started to cough. Blood flowed from his mouth, tinting his shirt bright red. Marina tried to mop up the blood with a thin scarf she was wearing – a futile effort. The flow was relentless. Between the bouts of coughing, we could see the blood spurting from his mouth. With the help of Marina, he stood up, holding his chest with both hands, his face contorted with pain. After taking a few steps towards their flat, he collapsed only a few feet away from Ali Baba's Cave. Marina called his name repeatedly between sobs and shouts for help.

'We've got to get out,' Carlota whimpered. In our haste, Tom Thumb was left, forgotten, between the rafters.

'I'll call my dad,' I said.

We squeezed out of the Cave as quickly as we could, very much to Marina's surprise. Minutes later, my dad was on the scene, together with Dr. Coronel, whom he had collected on the way up.

Lunch was almost ready. I related what we had seen to my mother and the rest of the family. There was concern on everybody's faces and despair on my mother's. My father did not return for quite a while, which added to the uncertainty.

Later I learned that Don Cesar had a punctured lung caused by a broken rib. He also suffered from severe bruising to the forehead. His vision was blurred. According to Dr. Coronel, there was no point in taking him to hospital, so he decided to take care of him personally.

'Now you only go to hospital if you're about to die, and if you're not, they'll kill you there,' he stated, with the authority of someone who knows.

Miraculously, Don Cesar recovered within a few months, and while he was ill Carlota and I helped Marina to feed the pigeons.

The colourful *Tom Thumb* book was recovered and Marina made a well-guarded secret of Ali Baba's Cave.

Enrique's Execution

Juanito's flat, like Don Cesar's, also had a terrace. It was located at the top of another block in another street, which crossed ours at right angles, and near enough to be visible from our balconies.

We played a game that could be considered the predecessor of table football. With chalk, we drew a rectangle – though the lines were not always straight and equal lines – on the red quarry tiles that paved the terrace. The players were bottle tops, and the ball was a *real* (royal), a small round nickel coin with a hole in the middle, the purpose of which, according to my father, was to enable Little Mouse Perez to escape to safety from a pursuing cat.

This game consisted of hitting the real with a bottle top by propelling it with a flick of the middle finger, always aiming at scoring a goal. One go each was allowed at a time.

Fighter planes were rarely seen patrolling the sky, but on some occasions Juanito and I interrupted our game to watch the dogfights, a spectacle that we enjoyed immensely, unaware of the fatal consequences this could have. But what interested us more was the rat-tat-tat of the machine guns and the spurts of fire issuing from their barrels.

Luckily the pilots of either side seemed unable to hit the target and no aeroplane ever went down in flames before our eyes. This, according to an older boy, who must have been at least fourteen, was because the pilots were too stupid to aim properly. Hearing this, Juanito vowed to devise a method to curb this defect.

For us it was just a show, but a year later, when things were really heating up, taking cover when the plains invaded the sky become a priority.

Juanito's mother, near apoplectic, would come out in a panic to fetch us in. Admonitions of 'No more football on the terrace before the war ends' would follow. Then the help of the Divine Providence was requested. Not that the admonishing or the invocation of the Divine

Providence did any good. We pursued our games when Juanito's mother's nerves were soothed under the effects of a tila infusion.

At the Larrumbe school, things became gloomy. Doña Amalia and her daughter, Maria Paz, donned black dresses. Not an even hint of a smile showed on their lips. They both tightly held a handkerchief that travelled to their eyes to wipe out tears. Doña Amalia's voice was often inaudible. After a few days of immersion in this heavily darkened atmosphere, the school was closed for a few days.

The news that Enrique, Doña Amalia's seventeen-year-old son, had been detained and subsequently executed soon spread around the neighbourhood. It was a bitter turn to an already bloody situation that had to be accepted without protest to avoid following him to the grave.

Enrique was apprehended for supposedly making the fascist salute by raising his right hand. This was a ridiculous accusation to make against a young man who was trying to attract the attention of a friend across the street, but it was an indication of how explosive the situation had become. The fascist salute, the hallmark of the National Falange, similar to the salute in Hitler's Germany and Mussolini's Italy, could gain you a bullet through the head, with or without interrogation.

When we returned to school a veil of sadness hung over us all. In the middle of a reading, Carlota wept inconsolably, joining Doña Amalia in her own tears, making it impossible to decipher what she was saying. Under normal circumstances, Carlota would have been reprimanded, but this time Maria Paz, handkerchief at the ready, got her to blow her nose and wipe her tears.

Juanito, sitting closer to me than ordinary, perhaps to find some comfort in my nearness, intermittently whimpered. I remained silent and observant, wishing tears would come to my eyes.

But the hero of the day was, without the slightest doubt, El Militino. When midmorning approached, time for his chronometric gut to erupt, he left the desk and swiftly gained the classroom door and disappeared, to return moments later, a little too soon, bringing with him a whiff of the reason for his exit. It was an extraordinary act of deference towards Doña Amalia in her hour of grief.

Slaughter

Preparations were underway for a long resistance to the Nationals, whose campaign was meeting with success in several regions. A committee was formed to deal with the safety of the block. Several occupants were selected. Amongst them were Dr. Coronel, two unknowns, and Carmina's father, Don Ricardo, his main qualification that of having been born in Catalonia, a north-eastern region where the support for the Reds was strong. But the head of the committee was Fernando overpowering scarlet, who later would become a machine-gun sergeant.

Finding shelter against air raids and possible attacks at ground level was of paramount importance. There was no basement in our block or in any of the surrounding buildings. The nearest underground station, Diego de Leon, was some fifteen minutes away, too far to be considered.

The space designated for shelter had originally been reserved for shops that, with the advent of the revolution, never materialized. A number of roller shutter doors made with corrugated metal, put in place for that purpose, were extremely vulnerable to riffle or even pistol bullets. The best solution the committee came up with was to reinforce the main walls at street level with sand sacks placed on the inside.

Two of my older brothers, together with other neighbours, were roped in for the job of filling the Hessian sacks with sand from a nearby field, now a development of luxury apartments. The sacks were then transported on an open lorry and subsequently stacked up ten high.

Reinforcing the ceiling was not possible, and in the event of a direct hit from the air, the whole block would have collapsed like a pyramid of matchsticks, trapping everybody underneath. However, that was not a thought that occupied our minds – they were already crowded with more vivid experiences.

Sirens came into operation fairly early at the beginning of the hostilities. When their strident voices broke the silence, it was time to rush down to the newly reinforced ground floor that masqueraded as a shelter.

My first trip to the Dungeon, as it was duly christened by Carlota, took place early one night when I was fast asleep. I still remember the strange sensation of being snatched out of bed by my father and propelled down the stairs, semi-naked, to join the people who had beaten us in the race to safety. Through sleepy and watery eyes I saw my clothes in a bundle under my father's arm.

Moments later, Carmina arrived with her father, a mass of blonde hair covering her face. Always ready to help me, even with sleep still in her eyes, she came over to where I stood. 'Come, Manolo, let's put your clothes on.' She sat me on the floor next to her and patiently helped me get dressed. With one sock missing and no shoes, I soon went to sleep, my head propped on her shoulder, her hair tickling my face. What happened in the shelter or how I returned to bed, I will never know. But somehow that is a memory that I still savour all those years after.

Another safety measure applied to windows. The glass could easily shatter with the force of the explosions. To ward this off, Fernando, brandishing the stick of authority like a newly victorious emperor, decreed all glass was to be covered with strips of paper placed vertically and horizontally. This was a tricky and messy operation; in the absence of adhesives, the strips had to be glued to the windows with an ominous kind of paste known as *engrudo,* made by mixing flour and water. Now, a few strips of masking tape would do the job in a fraction of the time. But that was a luxury beyond our reach, as the flour was to become.

To tighten the relationships of the community, Fernando decided that neighbours were to work on such an important venture in teams of three. Don Ricardo, as a prominent member of the committee, had carte blanche to choose his team. At Carmina's request, my family and Dr.Coronel's were chosen in preference to Carlota's, anticipating some improper use of the engrudo. We started our task by securing the doctor's windows. Carmina and her mother cut the strips, the doctor's wife mixed the engrudo, and two of my older brothers pasted and hung the strips. I was responsible for bringing old newspapers from the bottom of a cupboard to the table where the activities took place.

The operation, which was running smoothly, was interrupted by the sound of the doorbell. When it was ignored once, it repeated itself a second time, with an extra-long ring.

Carlota had her finger still on the bell push when Doña Carmen answered the door.

'Come in, young lady. Something told me it must be you,' she said with some hesitation, as if trying to choose between letting her in or sending her away.

'I've come to help with the pasting,' she said with a glint in her eye and an eager look at the goings-on on the table headquarters of the great venture.

'You can help Manolo bring the papers from the cupboard.'

It was not a very interesting job. She wanted to paste, and paste she would do. An air of unease started to circulate, fanned by low uttered whispers of 'Don't let her anywhere near the paste.' Carlota, unfairly branded as a mischief-maker, was totally misunderstood. All she wanted was to participate in the activities of the moment, often with too much zest.

Carmina, anticipating a revolt at Carlota's hands, took action. 'We can make a hat for Manolo, and you can stick the corners with engrudo.'

A wonderful idea! We sat on either side of Carmina, and with a full page of the *Informaciones,* an evening paper, we made a pointed hat for Carlota to complete with a few strokes of a thin brush dipped in the paste. I observed her happy face, her tongue wetting her lips as she brushed. When the corners were dry, the pointed hat was put on my head.

'There,' said Carmina with a smile, 'you look like a general.'

'I want to do something else,' announced Carlota with a mischievous smile.

She rolled a long piece of paper into a conical shape and then, the slightly dripping brush in hand, smeared my nose and placed the cone on it.

'Now you look like Pinocchio,' she said, and we all joined in with her contagious laughter. I did not say much. Watching my friends merrily laughing was enough for me.

After intense work, all the windows were duly covered in artistic criss-crosses, ready for the explosions to come. But in our minds, it was more ready to play noughts and crosses, if only chalk would work on glass.

The following day, Don Ricardo's windows were done by the same team. Ours were done the day after, in the absence of Carlota, whom my mother suspected to be a spy on the make.

Once the shelter and the windows had been dealt with, the committee focused on the approaching winter and the women were given the task of knitting sweaters for the soldiers. Again we all participated. Several women, including my older sisters, gathered in Doña Carmen's flat, mainly in the evenings, and while they knitted, the conversation flowed, embraced by the murmuring background of the Pilot radio. The women had coffee and Maria biscuits while we drunk hot chocolate.

I was not without a job in this venture, either. Sitting on a high chair, arms outstretched to keep the skein taught, I watched the wool being rolled into a ball. It amazed me how anybody could knit so fast, not needing to concentrate on the stitches as they passed from the needles into an ever-growing garment. It was a deed as near a miracle as I could ever imagine.

The war was sealed out of our minds then. For a few hours, no thoughts about explosions, air raids, interrogation and torture, executions, and the tragedy that had the country by the throat. Don Ricardo, tall and slim, modelled the sweaters for size, undoubtedly thinking of his son Ricardo, who had been called up to the front.

Don Ricardo was a man who kept his thoughts to himself. He measured his words as if they were a commodity in short supply. He never made a statement that could be taken to favour one side or the other. His sense of direction kept him firmly on the ground. But there is a limit to what the human countenance can hide. With his only son on the front line, my uncle Jesus's face showed signs of suppressed anxiety, and rightly so. Ricardo was in the trenches around November 7, 1936, when the Republicans, persuaded by Russian communist agents, ordered the slaughter of some two thousand detainees who were transported from the Modelo and San Anton jails in Madrid to Paracuellos del Jarama. Where they were shot, their bodies were left to rot on the ground. Another lot of prisoners was taken to Torrejon de Ardoz, which later became an American base, to be shot directly in an open trench that only needed to be covered with the soil parked by its side. Later in life, much later, when the Spanish Civil War was forgotten and the Nationals maligned, I learned that the slaughter of those men was the gravest shame of the Republic and provoked an enormous international scandal.

Death Threats

My father continued to receive anonymous threats in letters. Later, when I was older, Uncle Fabian told me that the sender must have done this out of spite rather than as a serious threat to my father's life. The letters contained a tone of resentment and accusations the sender wanted to voice, but could not bring himself to do so face-to-face. But whether they were intended to express resentment or to convey a real death threat, they created an atmosphere of vigilance that added to the overall misery.

The strongest suspicions fell on Silvester, who had been behaving in a very offhand manner that contrasted with his always impeccable respect towards my father – often servile, according to Uncle Fabian. The letters were written in red ink on ordinary paper, wrinkled, as if they had been in the sender's pocket for a time. The writing was well formed.

This much I would learn later. But at the age of eight, all I knew is what I overheard my uncle say –something about letters on crumpled paper and red ink.

I shared the information with Juanito, whose eyes shone at their brightest as they customarily did when his brain engaged in a very special logic that was seldom challenged by grown-ups. 'You say the ink is red.'

I assented.

'Your dad has got red ink in his office, hasn't he?'

I assented again.

Juanito paused for effect.

'The assassin is using your dad's red ink. Don't you see?' He pronounced the word assassin with so much gusto that dribble issued from the corners of his mouth. Uncle Fabian had not mentioned anything about an assassin, but watching my friend in the full flight of discovery, I remained silent.

'We could easily discover who it is, Manolo.'

'How?'

'One of us can hide in your dad's office and wait there until the assassin comes.'

A great idea, but not without its drawbacks.

'The assassin will never come during the day,' I pointed out.

'One of us will have to stay there at night.'

'One of us?'

'El Militino, Carlota, you, and I are a team, aren't we?'

'We are.' I felt proud to be a member of the team.

After some thought, Juanito came up with the answer. 'El Militino is out on account of his farting. If the assassin arrives when he is exploding, he may come to a sticky end – and we don't want that to happen to our friend, do we?' Superb reasoning.

'I can't get out of the house because my dad locks the door after dark. You can't for the same reason.'

Juanito was right as usual.

'It only leaves Carlota. She can hide anywhere,' I ventured.

'And can come out of the flat without difficulty when her dad is on night duty.'

'Won't her mum hear her if she's going out?'

'No chance. She snores all night.' A reassuring thought.

Carlota was the obvious choice. I thought about what my mother said when she tarnished her as an apprentice spy and realized how very much on the ball Juanito was, having chosen her for such an important mission.

Juanito kept mulling over the situation. 'Red ink! A sure sign of an assassin. They always use red ink.'

My friend was always so knowledgeable! Our plan could not but succeed. Now we needed to wait until Carlota's father was on night duty. Her acceptance of the mission was taken for granted. A great honour had been bestowed on her. We were sure that with her ability, my dad would be saved.

We put our plan to Carlota during an outing to a field nearby where we used to go wall lizard catching. Juanito was an expert catcher, who rarely allowed the creatures to slip out of his hand. Once one was caught, El Militino would proceed to stuff it with great flair. He did this like an accomplished surgeon, having learnt his skill from a family friend, a taxidermist whose flat contained beautiful specimens of stuffed birds and small animals. El Militino spent countless hours watching him work.

Before the lizard's tummy was split, its head would be dipped into a small bottle of surgical spirit that I brought from home. The surgical spirit worked instantly as a general anaesthetic. The cutting was done with a razor blade from El Militino's dad's shaving kit, and its innards were replaced with a piece of cotton wool impregnated with surgical spirit. Carlota would do the sewing. El Militino conducted himself with great seriousness and surprising cleanliness, not allowing himself to break wind, which, in the open, he could have done with impunity.

Juanito explained to Carlota what was expected of her. A very long silence followed during which she turned her head from left to right too many times for all of us to get worried. I could see that she did not think it such a great honour. Eventually she stamped her foot. 'Why doesn't El Militino do it?'

'You know why,' Juanito uttered in a low voice in order not to offend El Militino. He pointed at his belly. An unpredictable gut can exempt one from dangerous duties!

But Carlota was not that discreet. 'Perhaps if he stayed off cabbage and garlic during the day he could do it.'

El Militino's mother would never be a party to that, as she believed her son's rosy cheeks were precisely the product of her cooking, which was often supported by an extra portion of red kidney beans to ensure total energy. A lethal combination for those in close proximity. Reflecting on this point after so many years, I am sure she must have been right. I cannot remember my friend ever being ill. In fact, the whole family were the finest example of rude health.

After a while, Carlota felt she was letting us down. As a prelude to crying, tears welled in her eyes, then rolled down her face and into her pursed lips. I gave her a precious handkerchief that Carmina had embroidered with my name. The three of us wanted her to stop crying but said nothing.

'I'm scared,' she bubbled. 'I've been having nightmares since Manolo and I saw Don Cesar bleeding in the terrace.'

We sat on the ground. Juanito and El Militino put their arms around her shoulders while I watched them, searching my mind for something to say.

'I'm scared,' she repeated, 'scared of the dark. But I'll do it. I'll do it for Manolo's dad.' Then she put my handkerchief in the little pocket of her blouse for comfort.

A true friend. A hero in my heart.

Lentils and Potted Cat

Months had passed. The situation had worsened. We were now fully acclimatised to the horrors that started on July 18th, to such an extent that the status quo seemed to be normal, in spite of what we remembered from peacetime.

Food had not been plentiful for a long time, but now its scarcity translated into hunger. Keeping even a pitiful stock of food could cost dearly, as the secret police could burst into anybody's home when least expected, and hoarders would be severely punished, their hoard confiscated. But, contravening the direct orders of the government decree and at her own peril, my mother managed to get a few tins of corned beef, sardines, and sundry preserved fish and some rice and lentils. Later, when there was nothing else to eat, lentils would be referred to as Negrin's pills. Negrin, according to my knowledge, was a general fighting on the Red side.

Bombs continued to fall. Hand grenades were thrown at the supposed hiding holes of the Nationals, who were the enemy within, according to the Reds. Fear had everybody in its grip on all sides.

'One day this war will end,' Uncle Fabian was in the habit of saying. I always waited for him to finish the phrase. But he never did, just cast his eyes down and swallowed hard.

Uncle Fabian often reminded me that the times when we could go for a walk without the fear of crossing a stray bullet's path were now over. To crown it all, he was suspected to sympathize with the 'enemy', for the mere fact of being a co-owner of Montero Bros., and therefore a capitalist and for this reason, was in fear of being liquidated.

Uncle Fabian was a very special character. Without a doubt, he was too kind and weak for this world, possessing a resilience that kept him in good stead in dangerous situations and often behaving like a child who never grew up. Maybe for this very reason, he shared his secrets with me, secrets that a man in his middle years would have kept to himself.

Carmina was a big girl. Any girl who was two years older than me was a big girl. She had golden hair made into a plait that hung down her back like a luxuriant brocade. She could wrinkle her nose like rabbits do. And she did that inadvertently sometimes, sometimes to amuse me. I would watch her face patiently until it happened. Then, prolonged, happy laughter would follow. On some occasions, there was a price I had to pay.

'Oh, do it again, please. Just once more time,' I pleaded.

'Only if you plait my hair for me.' She pretended to play hard to get. But a low mellow tone betrayed her game. There was nothing I liked more than that. And like her, I would pretend.

'Do I have to?'

'Yes,' she said firmly.

'But nobody must see me do it.' I must have blushed at the thought of being made fun of.

So, we would go to a quite corner of the flat and there she would sit down while I, standing behind her, let my fingers weave the golden strands.

What we were up to was no secret to Uncle Fabian, who had seen us by chance on some occasions. He would say innocently, 'My! My! Who's done your plait today? It looks better than ever.'

'I do it myself, Uncle Fabian,' she would fib. He was not her uncle, but Carmina enjoyed referring to him as such, if only to share him with me.

Carmina and I had witnessed the horrors of the war often enough. Our baptism took place one morning when, hiding behind a tree, we saw the milicianos kick a nun to death.

'Don't look, Manolo. Don't look.' We were frozen by fear. Her voice still rings in my ears.

That happened when I could still feel fear like any other child, man, or woman. But soon, fear was replaced by a spirit of survival. A subconscious need to stay alive, to take things as they came without giving too much thought to what was happening.

Later Uncle Fabian, holding us both in his arms, would explain, 'That's the Reds for you.'

I could not but wonder what things would be like when the war ended, as I hoped it would. Uncle Fabian said it would often enough, and I was sure he must be right.

We had been surviving on lentils for some months, accompanied by maize bread, yellow and hard, almost inedible.

On lucky occasions, this diet was supplemented by a supreme delicacy – potted cat in fried tomato sauce, if we were doubly lucky.

'It's as good as hare,' Uncle Fabian would say.

With great skill, sharpened by compelling hunger, he hunted the felines in the early hours of the evening before the curfew started. A refined persuasion and a small Hessian sack, into which his prey went for a safe journey home, was all the equipment needed. Because of this, the population of itinerant cats in the neighbourhood dwindled. He showed no mercy. If a cat came within reach of his hands, it ended in the pot.

One evening, just after bagging a fat specimen, a stocky man hiding most of his forehead under a black hat grabbed his arm. Uncle Fabian recognized him as an agent of the secret police who frequently patrolled the neighbourhood.

'Out of our hiding hole so near curfew time, are we?' He flashed a sarcastic smile. 'If I find you around here in another ten minutes I'll have to run you in, won't I?' His sarcasm was mounting. And then, looking at the sack alive with the protesting animal, he asked, 'What have you got there?'

Uncle Fabian thought quickly. 'It's my Pirracas. My cat. He escaped. Went out looking for food.'

'That's no more your cat than I'm Comrade Stalin, you liar! Let him go before I put a bullet through your head.' His sarcasm turned into rage.

The secret police had unquestionable powers. Crossing them was temerity. Uncle Fabian was well aware of that.

'Papers,' the agent shouted, still maintaining a painful grip on his arm.

Uncle Fabian produced his identification papers.

'I see you're waiting to appear before the Purging Tribunal on charges of co-operating with the enemy. I seem to have made a lucky find,' blurted the agent, his face glowing with sadistic anticipation.

No more was said. The agent released his hold with a violent push and Uncle Fabian returned home empty handed and with a belly full of fear. That encounter was enough to remind him of the modus operandi of the secret police.

A car would stop outside a block in the night. Out of it would alight four men, and those four men would climb the stairs, stop outside some victim's flat, then a fierce knocking would rattle the door. Accusations of co-operation with the enemy would be enumerated. The beginning of the end! A short journey to a ghetto would follow. Then interrogation. Beatings. Torture. Quite likely death. It was often a welcome death for the victim.

'Any day now they'll come and get me,' he said to me in a trembling voice.

Later, I confided in Carmina. 'That red cockroach hurt Uncle's arm.' I was careful not to mention my uncle's fears. That would make her sad or even cry. And when she cried, I would feel like crying too. But men don't cry. I knew! I knew that men do not cry. 'Will God punish him for hurting Uncle?'

'He sure will. When he dies, he'll go to hell with Satan.' Carmina was knowledgeable about the afterlife.

'And will Satan prick him with his poker?'

'He sure will.'

'And will he suffer?'

'He sure will.'

'Are all the Reds bad?'

'They sure are!'

'And will God punish them all?'

'He sure will.'

Hard times had taught me to be resourceful. There was nothing I would not tackle to meet a need or for the sake of adventure. Often Carmina and I had been in danger of losing our lives.

Things came to a pitch when the supplies of food to the shops dried up.

'We're down to our last handful of lentils,' my mother told the rest of the family.

'We can get some in the Army stores.'

The Army stores were well guarded. Trespassers could be shot without ceremony.

'Carmina and I can go and get some there.'

'Too dangerous. You'll do no such a thing.' Uncle Fabian must have felt an icy shiver down his spine. 'If the sentry sees you, he'll shoot you.'

'He won't see us, Uncle. Carmina and I have been there many times. We know how to get in.'

We had played around the perimeter of the Stores before. But getting in was quite another matter, as there was no other way than to squeeze through the barbed wire.

The foraging operation was prepared with precision. Uncle Fabian took charge. He would follow us and wait in a safe place to escort us home.

My mother lengthened my trouser pockets to reach to my shoes, open ended at the top so that they could easily be filled with the coveted lentils.

Likewise, Carmina's mum made a pocket of sorts in her skirt.

For a few days, the unrest in Madrid, a Red stronghold from the beginning of the conflict, reached boiling point. A variety of political factions and rebel groups sprang up from time to time, giving way to sporadic shootouts when least expected.

As planned, we walked around the perimeter until we found a small hole through which we could enter. The barbs scratched me, but there was no time to feel pain.

A summer storm had been brewing all day. It started to rain. Torrential rain. In a few moments, we were soaked to the skin.

Once we were inside the perimeter, getting into the warehouse was easy. At first the place appeared to be deserted, but we soon saw many soldiers who were, luckily, sheltering from the rain in their quarters.

The warehouse was like a gigantic horn of plenty with sacks of provisions piling up, all marked with the commodity they held. Potatoes, lentils, rice, even bread and eggs, packed in paper bags resting on shelves at the far end.

'We mustn't be seen by the soldiers.'

'They won't come out of the shelter while it rains.'

Carmina was always reassuring. Quickly I filled my pockets with lentils and Carmina put a few rolls of bread in her skirt.

Once our clothing was loaded, it was time to scram. Swiftly, out of the warehouse and through the barbed wire we went. The rain, now accompanied by thunder and lightning, continued to fall even more relentlessly than when it started.

A deafening noise that repeated itself rumbled.

'What's happening? That's not thunder.'

'It's hand grenades. And bullets,' Carmina said in a whisper.

A rebel group opened fire in the proximity of the perimeter. The sound of explosions came increasingly near.

'Get down on the ground,' said Carmina, trembling.

'They're attacking the stores.'

From where we were lying, we could see the soldiers' helmets. Fire issued out the barrels of their rifles. Shouts of horror mingled with the noise of exploding hand-grenades.

The military stores were being stormed. The soldiers were caught by surprise. The attack only lasted a few minutes.

'We can now go,' we said in unison.

Used to this kind of happening, we started to crawl away from the scene with our precious loot. It was not easy for us to move, me laden down with lentils and Carmina having to hold on to her skirt so as not to loose her precious catch.

Suddenly the battle started again. A machine gun opened fire on the rebels from inside the compound. There was a fierce response of hand grenades. And a skirmish that appeared to have come to an end only minutes before, turned into a ferocious confrontation.

'Down! Down! Stick to the ground, Manolo.' Carmina put her arm around my shoulders, pressing me down into the wet earth.

Bullets were now buzzing around us. Shrapnel was falling everywhere. We remained where we were, bodies flat against the muddy ground. We stayed like this, not knowing what to do, and just waited for the fire to cease.

There was no sign of Uncle Fabian; for all we knew, he could be dead. I do not remember how long we remained there, wet and shivering with cold, but it felt like endless hours.

At long last the skirmish came to an end, and dazed as we were, we made our way in search of Uncle Fabian, guided by instinct rather than remembering how to get to the meeting place, which was as close to the perimeter as he thought prudent for him to wait.

The perimeter was situated on open fields where small bushes grew in profusion. Today, in contrast, blocks of flats have sprung up after years of construction.

We looked everywhere for Uncle Fabian and found him in a pool of rainwater, covered in mud, and quite unrecognisable. For a time we stood next to him and wondered whether he was dead or alive.

'He's moving his eyes!' I shouted.

'Uncle.' Carmina knelt next to him and attempted to pull him by the arm.

That was enough for him to stir. With some difficulty, he sat up on the ground and looked at us with surprise.

'Where are we?' he said.

'We came to the stores to get some food.' This was a clarion call that brought him back to reality.

'Did you get it?'

'We did.'

'Bravo!'

When he stood up, we realized that the back of his shirt was bloodstained.

'I must have been hit by shrapnel,' he said in a pained voice. Then, like he had said so many times, had added, 'One day this war will end.'

Sicknesses

Things were getting more difficult at home. My brother Jesus was called up and sent away. Luckily, he was assigned to Auxiliary Services on account of his stomach. He had a condition known to the family as dropped stomach, which, according to my parents, was due to his height. I remember him as very tall, thin, and possessing a large nose. He was my mother's favourite due to his gentle nature. News from him reached us intermittently. Because of his ability to draw, he had been assigned to the topography wing of his unit. He made friends easily, and according to his letters, he was not unhappy. But he was away from us. We missed him.

My mother, a great devotee of Saint Anthony of Padua, entrusted my brother to him and was sure the Saint would keep him out of danger. Saint Anthony had got my mother out of trouble many times. I knew this because I often heard her praying aloud, thanking the Saint for this or that and requesting things she needed. I never knew whether he performed or not, but I did know that my mother had him trained like a retriever. If she lost something she could not find, a couple of Our Fathers to him did the trick.

My sister Maria had not been well for some weeks. She was unable to keep the food down. I heard the doctor say she suffered from gastro-enteritis, which in my kind of vocabulary meant constant trips to the loo and horrible belly aches. During the first stages, she was given rice water to bind the intestines. I prepared it for her. First, some rice was left to soak for a few hours. Then it was worked on with pestle and mortar. Afterwards, when the grains were pulverized, the water they had soaked in was added. Finally, the mixture was ready for Maria to drink.

This kind of emergency home medicine seemed to work for a while, but eventually Maria got worse and reached a stage at which her legs would not support her. I could hear the word 'dehydration', which I could not quite interpret until one day when Maria had taken a turn for the worse. The doctor came armed with an enormous bottle of a liquid that looked very much like water and injected it into Maria's leg. The liquid, a saline suspension as I learned later, worked wonders. Her face that had become parched was soon covered in beads of perspiration.

Maria took a long time to get well, but even after that, gastric problems continued to appear. A chronic condition, a spasmodic colon, remained for most of her life as a macabre gift of the war. Those were the days before antibiotics were available, at least where we lived. Sulphamids such as Sulfatalidin, a white tablet, and Edifeno, a brown one, were used to treat conditions such as Maria's. However effective, they gobbled up the red blood cells, leaving an open door to anaemia.

During Maria's illness, Michito stayed outside her bedroom. This was a sure sign that my sister was not well. I waited for the day when he would go in and sit at the foot of her bed. His incredible sixth sense would tell us then that she was better.

The Raven

On non-school days like Saturday and Sunday, I went to the terrace to feed the pigeons. Now that I was a little older, I knew that they could not read the numbers on the front of the nest, as Don Cesar had fibbed, but were guided by instinct to get to their own homes.

On top of the building I felt closer to the sky. Up there, there was often a gentle breeze that caused the clouds to move faster.

With the passing of months, I had become very close to Don Cesar and the flyers.

'Now you're bigger, you can have your own birds,' he told me one morning. There was nothing I wanted to hear more than that. 'You can keep them on the balconies. If your parents like the idea, I'll give you a pair.'

I was thrilled with the offer.

'Won't they escape?'

'Not if you build them a nest and put in it a container with water to drink and bathe and another with food to feed. I can give you a hand to get started.'

Our conversation was cut short with Carlota's appearance. She stood on the threshold of the terrace pointing at Ali Baba's Cave, our favourite hiding hole, where I joined her. There in the diffuse light that filtered through the gaps in the roof, she exuberantly uncovered her plan.

She was in a great mood, a sure sign that she was plotting something she should not be doing.

'My dad will be on dark work on Tuesday.'

She always managed to refer to things in a different way than everybody else – 'dark work' meant night duty to those outside our circle.

I thought that what Juanito and the rest of us had planned had died a natural death: we assumed that Carlota had agreed to mount guard in my father's office in a moment of bravado, and by the looks of it, her father was never going to be on night duty. On my part, I was not sure that my friend's reasoning was right, since many of his projects had failed, like the cylindrical frozen pee, to mention but one.

'I can hide in the cupboard where the papers are kept before the gates are closed. Then when everybody's gone, I'll come out and hide under your dad's desk,' she took a deep breath, 'and wait there until the assassin comes.'

She was excited beyond belief – a genuine sign of a spy in the making. Perhaps my mother was right. If I had known then about Matta Hari, I would have seen in my friend a budding one.

I started to think that Juanito's plan was not such a good idea after all. Also, Carlota's reckoning was full of flaws. Hiding in the garage before the gates were closed was not going to be easy, amen of exiting her home without her mother knowing. Also if the 'assassin' did not turn up that night, the operation would have to be repeated. Common sense tried to undermine the plan.

'But you'll be hungry.'

'I thought of that,' she said, her enthusiasm mounting. 'I'll take a banana and some chocolate with me.'

Carlota's body and soul ran on the dark stuff.

'And cold. You'll be cold. You may even sneeze or cough, and the assassin will know you're there. Then you'll be in trouble. He may even kill you.' Painting a black picture could not fail. But it did. My words spurred her on even more.

'I'll put on a thick blouse and my knee socks. Also, I intend to wear a mask so as not to be recognized.'

And when I thought I had heard everything, a final shot came after a short pause.

'I'll try to take my dad's pistol.'

I could picture her walking down the street struggling to hide the weapon under her skirt.

'Your dad's pistol? It's too big and heavy, and the trigger will be stiff.'

'Not *his* pistol. He gave my mum a smaller one. I heard them talking about it. They call it a lady's shooter. All small and silvery. I'm sure I can manage it.'

With this explanation, I began to like the idea. In my eyes, she showed courage beyond praise.

'There's one more thing I need.'

'Like what?'

'A name. All spies have a name.'

'With your disguise, you'd look more like a bandit.'
'Bandits also have a name. Let's think of one.'
'You could be called The Raven,' I proposed, thinking quickly.
'The Raven?'

I pointed at her hair, black and shiny like a raven's plumage. The name hit a perfect bull's-eye that propelled her hopping gleefully round the cave.

My mother was definitely right. Carlota was a spy in the making with all the necessary attributes.

After my initial excitement with her plan wore away, I started to feel uneasy. But when Carlota got into her head to do something, nobody was going to dissuade her. And if she was able to discover who the sender of the anonymous threats was, my dad would be grateful to her for having uncovered the mystery.

There was nothing else to do now but to wait till Tuesday.

The Raven's Pistol

On Sunday mornings, before the violence began, Carmina and I and the rest of the flock surrounding my mother would go to mass at the Augustines' church on the corner of our street. All in all, the 'flock', supplemented by cousins, friends, and occasionally Uncle Jesus, mustachio shiny with lacquer and redolent with the smell of *picadura*, a species of dark tobacco for rolling your own cigarettes, could be twenty strong. A show of unity marching on the pavement stretched from the main walls of the building to the curb.

On the way to the church, Carmina and I would play a guessing game trying to find out which colour chasuble the priest was going to wear, as according to Maria, there were chasubles of different colours to be worn on different days. She went to a lot of trouble to enlighten me on the significance of the colours. Her explaining, however erudite, did not sink in, probably because I was more concerned with guessing than with the reason for the changes.

When we reached the church, the saintly figure of Brother Ruperto would welcome us with open arms and a scattering of blessings. Then came the scramble for the pews as we advanced through the aisle. Altogether it was a perfectly planned military operation, with my mother in command. Seats for all of us were the reward when we arrived well in advance of the proceedings.

I never knew what went on during mass, but I felt happy sitting next to Carmina. I entertained myself watching the priest officiating, lifting his right hand and crossing the air at benediction time, then holding up the chalice as he had previously done with the host and drinking something from it. Red wine I was told it was. That made me wonder if his breath would smell like my father's did when he drank it occasionally during lunch.

Towards the end of the ceremony, if I ever showed signs of captivity in the rarefied atmosphere of the church, Carmina would hold my hand and whisper, 'Only a little while longer, Manolo.'

But that was in the past. Now, no going to church anymore. Not after the thousands of nuns, priests, and clergy in general had been and continued to be massacred. Not now that showing any religious inclination amounted to death.

So Sunday mornings were spent doing other things. And that Sunday, Don Cesar, Carmina, and I occupied ourselves in building a nest for the promised pair, whom we christened Scheherazade and the Sultan.

Our balconies had a wrought-iron structure of tall twisting vertical bars joined at the top by a banister-type rail. We ran several lengths of string across the bars to make an cage with an open top.

'When Scheherezade and the Sultan have little ones, that will keep them safe until they can fly,' Don Cesar explained.

A box resting on the floor, showing the number one at the front and with straw for floor covering, was designated as a breeding place.

'We number the nest so that the birds can find their home,' he said with a wink.

Two clay containers, one for water and one for food completed the project.

'We'll need to put something shiny to guide them back here until they have got used to their new location.'

We had the very thing, an old aluminium saucepan that had seen better days, now decorated with an array of holes at the bottom.

The idea of numbering the nests was a practical one, as when the pigeon population grew in numbers it became a must to keep tabs on the breeding frequency of the birds.

Later, as the war grew unbearably long and the scarcity of food constituted a permanent nightmare, our pigeons became manna from heaven. Although we got attached to them, in times of near starvation they became a much-wanted commodity on the plate.

Unlike taking them to be slaughtered by the embroiderer, as we had done with chickens before the war, two of my older brothers did the killing. Before experience taught them how, my brothers tried to cut their heads off with a pair of scissors, a method that was given up as unsuccessful. Don Cesar came to the rescue.

'Press hard on both sides of the chest and the birds will soon die of asphyxia,' he said, not without a sad concern in his voice.

Scheherezade and the Sultan soon settled in our balconies, and the whole family derived great enjoyment from watching them fly out of their new abode to tour around the close neighbourhood and return home without ever getting lost. Michito, after the first shock of meeting the new inhabitants of our balconies, became riveted to their activities and in time established a courteous friendship. We tested his good intentions by putting a morsel of his food in the birds' territory. If they tried to purloin it, he daintily would put his paw on their head as a friendly warning. It was enough evidence that they would live in harmony ever after.

That Sunday afternoon, when Don Cesar and Carmina had returned to their respective homes, I found a letter that Carlota had pushed through the bottom of the entrance door to our flat.

The letter, written in green crayon on an uneven scrap of paper, inside an envelope to match, read: 'Come to Ali Baba's Cave. Hurry,' signed, 'THE RAVEN'.

When I arrived I found my friend sitting on an upside-down bucket covered with a homemade cushion reading *Aladdin and His Wonderful Lamp*. There was another upside-down bucket and cushion for me next to hers. Each cushion had our name cross-stitched on it. Carlota the homemaker!

'My mum helped me with the stitching. She said that Ali Baba had seats like these in his cave.' A comforting thought!

'*Aladdin* is a wonderful story. I wish I had a lamp like his and that a genie would come to me when I wanted him to.'

Somebody had given her a beautifully illustrated copy of the *One Thousand and One Nights*, which we used to take turns reading aloud.

'Only two days till we discover the assassin.' Her enthusiasm had not waned. A genie... we badly needed one right now!

'See how I'm going to disguise myself.' She had brought a small wicker basket. The contents were covered with a red cotton cloth. After removing it, she proceeded to take several things out for me to see.

Exhibit one: A black eye mask similar to the one bandits like Dick Turpin wore. She put it on. Exhibit two: The cotton cloth with which she covered her head and part of her face.

I was mesmerised at her ingenuity.

'Tell me you know who I am, Manolo.'

But for a tell tale chocolate stain on her skirt, I would not have recognised her. 'You're the Raven.'

She danced around, and we both laughed.

'Now close your eyes,' she said in mysterious tones.

I did as I was told, and when I opened my eyes again I found her standing opposite me with a silvery pistol in her hand.

'The Raven!' I gasped.

'Hands up, you pig!' she shouted in a guttural, raspy manner.

I stood still, looking at the mouth of the barrel.

'Hands up you pig,' she repeated. 'If you move I'll shoot you, you pig!' she continued.

I put my hands up and dared not move. I had seen scenes like this in real life, and I'd witnessed the impact of a bullet in a man's chest and how that man slumped to the ground in an instant.

Carlota put the gun down and removed her eye mask and scarf.

'Was that OK?'

'You scared me fartless.'

'That's what I'll say when the assassin comes.'

'What will you do if he doesn't do as you say?'

'I'll shoot him. Nobody messes with the Raven.'

'Imagine you kill him.' She was so convincing I was at a loss for something to say.

Carlota thought for a moment. 'We'll have to transpose the body.' (This meant dispose of the body, for those outside the Raven's circle.).

'Who's going to do that?'

'We'll get Carmina to help us.'

She had obviously thought of everything, including me. Although I was thrilled with her plan, I would never have wanted dear Carmina to get mixed up with murder.

I must have looked worried. I was perplexed to say the least. Carlota sniffed that.

'It'll be OK, Manolo, you'll see. I want to show you something else.' She picked up the basket and showed me a banana, a packet of wafer biscuits, and a whole tablet of El Gorriaga chocolate. 'Emergency rations for Tuesday night.'

The Raven was determined! I revelled in her disguise, especially the way she held the pistol.

'Could it not have gone off when you were calling me a pig?'

'Never. It's got a catch. See. I'll show you.'

Saying that, she started to brandish the pistol with relish. Suddenly, much to our surprise, it went off. A bullet bore a hole in the roof of our hideout, showing a small circle of sky through it. We were startled. Almost immediately, hurried footsteps stopped outside Ali Baba's Cave.

'Carlota, are you in there?' Don Cesar's woman asked nervously.
'Yes, Doña Marina. Manolo is here with me.'
'Anybody else?' Now there was fear in her question.
'No, Doña Marina, only us.'
'What's that smell?'
'It's nothing, Doña Marina. We're just playing cops and robbers.'

But the unmistakable smell of gunpowder did not go unnoticed. Although it was not unusual in the climate of the revolution for snipers to shoot sporadically, Don Cesar's flat was only a few feet away from the roof terrace and almost adjoining our hideout, making a bullet noise too close for comfort.

Carlota and I looked at each other sheepishly. Minutes later, Doña Marina returned with her mother in tow. Difficult times for the two of us loomed on the horizon.

El Responsable

After a mild and capricious, changeable autumn, the winter arrived quite suddenly, before its due time – a prerogative of the Madrid weather.

As a result of the episode in Ali Baba's Cave, Carlota's mother kept her prisoner. The eye mask and red cotton cloth were confiscated and the silvery shooter kept under lock and key. She was only allowed out to go to school, and the return home was closely monitored.

My mother reinforced her belief that the Raven was a spy in the making. Even the pseudonym gave her away. San Antonio de Padua was called upon in prayer and spoken to in no uncertain terms, demanding that that 'child of the devil' be kept away from her Manolo – A kind of celestial injunction to keep Carlota's dangerous influence at bay.

Juanito's and El Militino's admiration of Carlota reached the very top of the scale, and the latter felt obliged to present her with a banana from his father's shop.

'Only a temporary hitch,' Juanito said. His ingenuity never defeated by the 'occasional' obstacle. 'We'll find out who the assassin is,' he reassured me.

But my father kept on getting threat after threat and so decided to tell El Responsable as Uncle Jesus advised. 'A long shot, but worth trying.'

El Responsable, whose name was Fulgencio, had established a kind of friendship and respect for my father once he realized he was a hard-working man like any other minion of the proletariat. He admired most that my father, before staining his social principles by becoming a 'capitalist', had been oppressed by those whose main asset was their wealth. It is quite possible that at some time or another my father must have related to him that for some years he had been the chauffeur to some big cheese of the nobility who, in his will, recompensed him for his services, making it possible to finance Montero Hermanos.

I am sure that tears must have come to Fulgencio's eyes when he heard my father's humble beginnings. I can visualize him saying something like, 'What you must have suffered under the clutches of those exploiters of the workers.'

Aided by his knowledge of my father's past suffering under the boot of the bloodsucking oppressors, Fulgencio occasionally bypassed the obstacles of his socio-communistic hang-ups and referred to my father as Don Salvador, his Christian name, rather than as Comrade Salvador.

When El Responsable was shown the scraps of paper where the threats had been written, his face must have contorted. 'There's some *hijo de puta* amongst us. This is not how the Regime wants to build a new Spain.' Then with resounding authority in his words, reinforced by waving the evidence in the air, he continued. 'I shall get to the bottom of this, and when I find the bastard I'll smash his *cojones* with the butt of my pistol.'

It was not an idle promise and was followed by a blaspheming litany that included many favourites of the language of Cervantes, such as *Me cago en Dios* (I shit on God.) and *Me cago en su puta madre* (I shit on his whore of a mother.). A few friendly and reassuring slaps on Comrade Salvador were followed by 'You just leave this to me, Don Salvador.'

Fulgencio was a man of action, and within a few minutes of this most engaging scene, he had gathered the whole of the working force, about thirty strong. 'I'm not going to mince words. Comrade Salvador has been sent threats on his life. I'm sure the culprit is amongst us. I'll give that bastard one hour to come forward and explain himself.'

A deadly silence followed. The hour passed. No one came forward. The work force was assembled again. 'If the *cabron,* (the bastard) who has done this thinks he's going to get away with it, he'll be putting a bullet hole in his own head.'

El Responsable chose several of his favourite minions, Julian and Silvester included, on account of having worked in the garage since its creation. Tables were set up. Paper, pens, and red ink made available and one by one everybody, family and non-family members alike, were ordered to copy the latest anonymous threat in order to find the matching handwriting. Whether there was any logic in this, it was worth giving it a whirl.

Nobody was identified by this operation, which was managed with great determination and accuracy, but the anonymous threats stopped. Fulgencio's self-confidence increased, and he strutted like an overfed peacock around the premises for days.

Uncle Jesus related these events to me, and I told my friends. A truculent expression appeared on Juanito's face. 'That would have been my number two plan.'

'Would El Responsable have shot the cabron if he had found out who it was?' asked El Militino, a concealed wish of revenge in his question.

'The Raven would have discovered the assassin much better.'

'She was robbed of the chance.'

Carlota, under house arrest, would have enjoyed our solidarity.

The Explosion

Carlota's curfew was lifted after many days of imprisonment. Juanito, who appointed himself our leader without saying a word, suggested that to celebrate the occasion, the four of us should go to El Canalillo to watch the pebble fight between two enemy gangs of the bigger boys. The boys were at least fourteen or fifteen years old; this seems like a huge age difference when you are only nine. The gangs were captained by El Serrucho (The Saw) and El Pirata (The pirate). The foot warriors under their command were armed with catapults, and El Serrucho and El Pirata were armed with slings.

El Canalillo was an open field where blackberry bushes, nettles, briar, and high grass competed with each other amongst mounds of muddy earth and stones and definitely small pebbles ideal for catapult ammunition. Bigger stones were used in the slings, which could cause real harm if they were to hit you on the head. Luckily, good aim with the slings was difficult, but more than once we saw the occasional warrior retire from the fight because of a bloodied head.

Those fields took the name El Canalillo (little canal) from a small canal running along its upper side, fenced off by lines of barbed wire supported by concrete posts. Though my mother forbade me to go there, it was our favourite place for catching small lizards. The Hessian sacks used to protect the ground level zones of the blocks of flats where we lived were filled with the soft earth from these fields.

The main attraction of El Canalillo was a kind of natural cave, not unlike a grotto, made with compacted mud and excavated by gipsies to form a shelter. Other children, normally older, used to play in the cave, and so did we when they were not about. On rainy days, which were rare, chunks of the roof came down, splashing liquidy mud about.

El Canalillo was quite close to where we lived, and that day, in great spirits for the return of Carlota, we walked down Castello, and across Maria de Molina to reach our destination.

We walked, arms resting on each other's shoulders, a happy four-link chain singing naughty songs. One of them was the best memory aid for the fives in the multiplication table, with lyrics composed by the four of us, now borderline obscene, then just words to make us laugh:

> Cinco por cinco, el Tio Francisco.
> Cinco por seis, con su mujer.
> Cinco por siete, se la mete.
> Cinco por ocho, por el chocho.
> Cinco por nueve, tiene un nene.
> Cinco por diez, otra vez.

Uncle Fabian lived in one of the blocks in Castello, and as a sign of respect, we lowered our voices when we passed by his place. I had not seen him since he was hit by shrapnel and laid up with wounds that refused to heal.

There was no stone fight when we arrived.

The alternative was to play a Tabas game. The *taba* (knucklebone) is the bone part of the knee joint of a sheep. Carlota had come prepared bringing a taba with her, without a doubt rescued from the remains of a lamb stew, wrapped in the red cotton cloth she had put on as part of the Raven disguise. She was very proficient at this game, and invariably, she won.

The taba has four sides: a broad convex side called the belly; the opposite to this, called the valley due to its convexity; and the two narrow sides, one deeper than the other, called the king and the *verdugo* (executioner), respectively.

To start with, the taba is thrown. If it falls belly up, it is passed on to the next player. Whoever gets a king becomes one and can command any tasks he wishes, to be overseen by the verdugo. A valley means punishment as ordered by the king.

Sitting cross-legged in a circle, we started by drawing lots and I, having drawn the longest one, was the first to throw and got a belly. I passed the taba to Juanito, who got a dreaded valley. Punishment deferred until a king was found! El Militino threw another belly, giving Carlota the opportunity to grab the taba and submit it to a ritual the rest of us had seen many times: she blew on it, rubbed it on her palms many times, and finally muttered a secret command, after which she threw it and successfully got a king.

Her eyes shone with glee, and in her best commanding voice she ordered Juanito to pick up a nettle without being stung and bring it to her.

A prickly task! But knowing Juanito's inventiveness, we were curious to see how he executed the command. We all watched in wonder.

'Easy when you know how,' Juanito said smugly, and taking off his trouser belt, he wrapped it round the stem of the nettle, pulled it out of the ground, and presented it to the king.

We had a few more rounds and having got a valley, it was my turn to carry out a task. Carlota, inevitably having got a king, commanded me to gather blackberries. I knew she was waiting for me to get a valley, as being the tallest, I would return a better crop. The Raven's red cotton cloth came into play and I duly filled it with berries bursting with juice.

We stopped the game and concentrated on eating. Our feast was interrupted by a loud explosion followed by several minor ones and a column of thick black smoke that seemed to come from the direction of Nunnez de Balboa, where my father's workshop and garage were. The smoke was quite visible from where we were, as El Canalillo ran along the topside of an elevated rampart.

Time to return home, and quick! We were sure that Montero Hermanos had been hit by a bomb or, rather, several of them.

'Perhaps this is the assassin to kill Manolo's dad,' El Militino whispered in Juanito's ear in a low voice, but not quite low enough to prevent me from hearing it.

As before, we passed by Uncle Fabian's block. He was at the window and on seeing us, shouted, 'Manolo, go home, go home!'

A group of people hurriedly walking from the direction of the explosions commented loudly.

'Must be the garage,' said one.

'Couldn't be anything else...'

These comments unleashed all manner of scenes in my mind.

'If the silvery shooter hadn't gone off, the Raven would have found out who the assassin was, and this wouldn't have happened.' El Militino would not abandon his original idea.

'It's all my fault,' whimpered Carlota.

'The last threat sounded like the last chance.' Juanito was obviously in agreement. I remember hearing these words as if they did not refer to my father, but when we got near the crossroads where we lived and saw an ambulance from the Red Cross and a fire engine, I realized that what my friends were saying could well be true.

At home, my mother was in a terrible state praying feverishly to San Antonio de Padua and the whole of the celestial court, which made my fears grow. Her invoking some extraterrestrial power was not unusual on stormy days, which were plentiful, especially in the autumn when Santa Barbara was given priority over San Antonio. My mother would then find refuge in the hall, the only dark place in the house from which lightning could not be seen. Michito accompanied her there, managing to get under her feet, either with feline malevolence or simply by accident. Her hurried steps were peppered with 'He's going to claw me, he's going to claw me,' and he would have done so had she trodden on his precious tail.

But on that day, fear had taken over. El Michito, arching his back and snorting with disapproval, disappeared under a bed. My sister Maria scolded me as if I were responsible for what had happened. 'Where were you?' she asked sternly, not so much to satisfy her curiosity but to tell me off, whatever my reply would be.

And when I told her we were in El Canalillo, she found all manner of reasons why I should not go there. 'Those big boys are going to injure somebody with their stone fights. That cave is made of mud and one day is going to collapse on top of somebody and crush the person to death.' She was truly in full swing but her scolding seemed to do me good, and I reacted by accepting whatever happened, as I had been taught to do.

From our balconies, I could see a great commotion in the street: people milling around, some static, forming small groups, others going in the direction of the smoke that continued to reach for the sky in an amorphous column.

My mother, who at first had pledged an array of impossible things to the Saint, changed her tune when the smoke spread down our street, General Oraa, towards our block. She began issuing a litany of recriminations well outside the Catholic protocol, until a while later the Saint, true to form, performed one of his many miracles: An ambulance returned from the scene followed by El Benz, Klaxon blaring, with my father at the wheel. Relations were restored with the Saint, not without some recrimination for the unnecessary fright.

As night approached, more accurate news reached us. We stayed on the balcony, riveted to the activity in the street below, and saw Uncle Jesus returning home, limping badly and covered in muck. My father came back late into the night. I was already in bed, half asleep but alert enough to feel his comforting good-night kiss as he rearranged the bedclothes around my shoulders.

When I was older I learnt that there had been no bombs hitting the garage and that the explosions had occurred across the street in a laboratory where celluloid was made.

My father and my uncle Jesus gathered the working force to help the casualties before the fire brigade arrived. With the explosion, the front door of the laboratory flew across the street, smashing against the opposite block. Windowpanes became a shower of glass that spread all over. Flames transformed the building into a burning nightmare. Shouts of pain and for help added to the drama. El Benz was filled with the injured and so was an ambulance of the Red Cross as soon as it arrived.

Julian, Silvester, and several of our mechanics followed firemen into the building. Severely injured laboratory workers were rescued from the flames. Two men were found dead. One was a fireman; the other was one of our mechanics, nicknamed El Exaltado (hot-headed), who distinguished himself for his bravery.

Several days after the ordeal was over, Silvester told my father, 'You won't be getting any more threats, Don Salvador. El Exaltado had another anonymous threat in his wallet, and it was a final warning.'

In spite of that, my father always kept the revolver with him.

El Responsable put on a countenance of respect when referring to him and refrained from blaspheming according to the principle that you must not speak ill of the dead.

Of course the events of that day became a topic of conversation with my friends.

'I knew El Exaltao,' which was Exaltado in Carlota-speak, 'he had mad eyes.'

'Popping out like frog's.' El Militino was obviously in the know.

'Wish I had seen him myself,' Juanito joined in.

'What would you have done?' Carlota asked, stoking up the fire.

'I'd have gone into the garage and put a poison scorpion in his boot. That's what I would have done.' This would have been difficult, since there were no scorpions in Madrid and their closest relatives, *el alacran*, were not equipped with any lethal stuff.

We laughed at Juanito's ingenuity.

'Pity you missed your chance,' El Militino said in consolation. 'Now he's dead and will be eaten by worms.'

Somehow this remark triggered remorse in the rest of us. A few seconds of silence followed.

'Is it true that nails continue to grow when you're buried?' Carlota wanted to explore what happened in the grave.

'And the hair.' El Militino knew his physiology.

'And your soul goes black.' Juanito knew about the afterlife.

Uncle Jesus's Wounds

Carmina came down to our flat as she usually did to help me with my school homework. On that day, I practised calligraphy, which was done in an exercise book whose pages had narrow double lines for the small letters and a top, more distant line for the capitals.

We sat in the dining room at a round table of smooth dark wood, large enough to accommodate the whole family at meal times. According to Maria, it had belonged to our grand auntie Petra, who was always described as the personification of misfortune because she had been twice jilted at the altar in spite of her remarkable beauty. The table was assembled in two halves, supported by twin and single legs for stability. One of the legs was in the habit of working itself loose from time to time, until my brother Jesus stuck it together with a kind of hot glue that was notorious for its pungent smell.

Under Carmina's tutelage, I copied two whole pages.

'This is much better, Manolo. Next time you'll practice with a patagallo nib.'

Horror of horrors! A patagallo nib! Doña Amalia's favourite instrument of torture, which none of my peers could master. It earned us detention after detention – which we did not mind, as several of us were left together in a now-empty classroom for half an hour or so; little writing was done during that time. Instead, we spent most of the time on the construction of paper aeroplanes.

My mother was concerned about Uncle Jesus's injuries, so when the homework was done, Carmina and I were sent to see him. Uncle Jesus lived across the street, in a smaller flat than ours, with Auntie Ignacia and our cousin Jesusin (little Jesus), a short, extrovert-emaciated boy of perhaps fifteen. He was highly impressionable and very artistic; he could draw with pencil as well as paint with watercolours.

When we arrived, Uncle Jesus was sitting on his wing chair. One arm was bandaged and one trouser leg cut off halfway down the thigh, exposing a bandaged leg. His plight did not affect the pure majesty of his mustachios, which were waxed as ever and shiny under his large nose.

His arm had been burnt. To alleviate the scorched skin, Auntie Ignacia had applied picric acid, commonly known as yellow water, perhaps the only remedy available at the time. The leg had sustained a deep gash that had been smeared with iodine after being stitched up by a medic.

'You find me nursing my wounds. And very colourful they are too.' His broad smile matched his sense of humour. 'Yellow for the arm. Dark red for the leg. Almost like the flag of our country.' No mention of pain was made, but his occasional grimacing made me think he was dealing with it in the same stoic manner I was being brought up to behave.

Coal was almost impossible to obtain. People resorted to using coal dust instead. A simple technique made this possible. Damp newspaper sheets were combined with the dust and the mixture was made into a ball, ready for use in the kitchen range.

Auntie Ignacia enlisted our assistance to carry out such an important task, and supervised by Jesusin, we got on with the business of creating this innovative fuel. We had been so engrossed with our assignment that we failed to notice that Jesusin had left us alone. Knowing that he would never miss an opportunity to get into mischief, Carmina warned me in a whisper, 'He's up to something, Manolo.'

No sooner had she said it than Jesusin appeared, walking stealthily towards us in a cat-like, pussyfooting manner, his hands covered in the black stuff.

'You don't look like real coal kids. Real coal kids have black faces.'

Kneeling on the kitchen floor next to the range, we tried to get up and run away from him, but before we could escape, he ran his hands down our faces, blackening them.

'There,' he said with a truculent smile, 'Now you look real and so much prettier.'

'Idiota,' shouted Carmina, making for the door. 'I'll tell Uncle Jesus.'

The truculent smile disappeared. Telling Uncle Jesus meant punishment.

'I'll pay a penalty if you don't,' he pleaded, standing by the door to prevent our exit.

Carmina could not think of a hard enough penalty.

'I'll draw your portrait and we'll call it *The Coal Kids of General Oraa.*'

This was a fair proposition, especially for Carmina, who was chuffed with his drawings. So we went into his room and together we sat on the edge of his bed, a *cama turca* (a Turkish bed), entirely made of metal with tubular head and foot ends of arching chrome, painted in purpurine. The springless mattress was a mesh, to support a wool tufts-filled sort of palliasse. The bed could easily be taken apart in a matter of minutes. This was useful for ridding it of bugs, which in the hot summer months seemed to appear from nowhere to feed on the blood of the bed's occupant. It was common belief that the invading bugs were choosy as to the blood they preferred and stayed away from the less tasty specimens.

With no DDT, Auntie Ignacia set about the cremation of the bloodsucking blighters with an old piece of rag held at the end of makeshift wire forceps, impregnated in petrol. When this device, no doubt the predecessor of the flamethrower, was set alight, a crackling sound spread about the bedroom as the invaders and their larvae burnt. It was an extremely clean and efficient practice that is frowned upon in today's cotton wool society.

While being drawn, Carmina and I eyed the many odd things in the room. His pictures took up most of the wall space, many in China ink that glowed in the bright daylight. But it was his crystal set, with a lone headphone, that attracted our attention most. It was a mystery to me how by scratching the crystal with something as thin as a hair, the headphone came alive with music.

'There's more to it than that,' Jesusin explained. 'You also need an aerial to bring the airwaves to the set – and what a better one that the mesh mattress.' Although the explanation went over my head, I accepted that if it was one of his tricks it must be a good one.

Besides cremating bedbugs, petrol had other uses. One of my bigger sisters cleaned my father's suits with it. A cloth doily impregnated with the stuff and liberal rubbing made them as good as new at a time when dry cleaners, in their infancy, were thin on the ground and prohibitively expensive.

A puzzling oddity of his room was the display of danger from the electrical wiring. The light switch by the door, which had crumbled to exhaustion with use, had been replaced by an electric lighter. The electric light was composed of two narrow strips of metal, against which another piece of metal, not dissimilar to a thin pencil, with a wooden knob for a holder and a bit of cotton wool soaked in petrol was rubbed for instant ignition. It was also a free replacement for matches, which were in short supply, like most things. Next to the lighter, christened the Devil's Tail, were two bare wires in place of the light switch. Joining the wires activated the bulb, and this required a great deal of skill. As children, fear of electrocution or even of being shaken by the 110-volts current was never lodged in our thoughts. Not so in Auntie Ignacia's and Uncle Jesus's minds, who in a severe duet of soprano and basso profundo admonished Jesusin for joining the wires, but without any positive results.

Relying on electricity became a non-starter as soon as it began to be rationed. The power fluctuated from day to day. There were periods with no supply at all. At other times, especially late evenings, the current was so low that light bulbs just produced a faint glow.

Jesusin worked on the drawing for an hour or so. When he finished *The Coal Kids of General Oraa,* he wiped our faces with a flannel, leaving a conspicuous black spot on the tip of our noses, and sent us home.

The Catapult

The events of the previous days, although frightening, did not deter us from going to El Canalillo again. That was our private territory. There, the four of us felt more united than ever.

El Militino had a special 'assignment' from his mother, who wanted to present a relative with a stuffed lizard. Our friend was over the moon with the idea and gathered the three of us in a council of war.

'We've got to find a big one,' he announced.

'A big one? How big?' Carlota had misgivings about the size.

'The biggest we can find.'

'But the big lizards have teeth and bite. I don't want to be bitten.'

I could see Carlota was scared. So, I spread a little balm. 'My brother Rafael says that if you have a hanky and show it to the lizard he'll bite on it. Then all you have to do is to pull him by the tail and his teeth will come off in the hanky.'

There was a moment's deliberation amongst those present. None of us agreed with my brother's reasoning. We declared the motion null and void and laughed.

Juanito was more effective in dealing with Carlota's fear. 'Even if we wanted a great big lizard, we would not be able to find one here. Those live in some terrible place like La Patagonia.'

More laughs. La Patagonia. It sounded funny. Where was that?

We searched for our lizard without luck. But Carlota, who was walking a few paces in front of us, found something half buried in the ground. It was a catapult – a proper one, a metal sort of fork with wide red elastic bands. A real beauty.

'Let me have it. Catapults are not for girls. I'll show you how it works,' said Juanito.

This comment was a breach of protocol by Juanito that encouraged Carlota to show him what a girl could do. It also allowed her to show a bit of bravado to compensate for her show of fear regarding the big lizard. Ignoring Juanito's words, she picked up a pebble, loaded her weapon, aimed at a nearby tree, and shot with the precision of William Tell. Then, she gracefully passed the catapult to Juanito.

We all had a try. The catapult passed from hand to hand many times, but none of us could best Carlota's aim. Behind the tree we had chosen as our target, there were bushes that partly covered a small path leading to an elevated part of the field. This part of the field was ideal for the pebble fights between the bigger boys, who planned this activity like a military operation.

Before the *drea* (pebble fight), El Serrucho, El Pirata, and with their foot warriors gathered like two football teams and tossed a coin to choose territory. The lucky ones moved to the higher ground. The drea would then begin, only to finish when one of the contenders was covered in blood, normally from an impact to the head.

We spent some time absorbed in our new game. Our ability grew with every shot – except for El Militino, whose mind was on his assignment. Inadvertently he moved away from us.

'He's gone to catch his lizard,' Juanito said.

'He'll find the lizard where the rocks are. That's where they hide. When the sun shines they come out to sunbathe.' Carlota was knowledgeable about lizard's habits.

I knew he would return with his pray. So he did.

'Got him!' An effusive El Militino showed us a wriggly specimen still imprisoned in his hand, soon to take residence in a flask with surgical spirit. The flask regularly accompanied El Militino, as he was always on the look out for creatures to dissect. 'I'll stuff it at home.'

Normally he did this in El Canalillo so that we could all participate in the operation, but this time, now that he had got his prey, he wanted to try his skill with the catapult.

'It's dead easy. Just look at the tree and let the pebble go.' Carlota, the shooting instructor, said.

El Militino did as he was told. The pebble flew well past the tree.

Then some very angry shouts came from behind the bushes.

'*Joder!*' which meant 'fuck', '*Me cago en Dios!*' (I shit on God)

The shouts continued in a crescendo. More 'Joder!' and more blaspheming. There was a rustle of branches, and then the source of the shouts appeared, one hand covering his left ear, the other holding a sling. It was none other than El Serrucho, with a menacing look about him.

His ear was bleeding. Time for us to stay calm and not to panic. The word panic was absent from our dictionary.

'You'll pay for this, *cabrones.*' (bastards). An idle threat? We exchanged glances as he walked away.

'I know why he's called El Serrucho.' Carlota whispered trying to diffuse the tension of our predicament. 'His front teeth are all jagged, just like a saw,' she explained, too impatient to wait for questions.

We got ready to return home when a large stone whistled through the air to land with a thud on Juanito's eye.

'*Joderos!*' El Serrucho wrapped the sling around his hand and, squatting on his haunches, continued a barrage of insults.

Juanito was too proud to scream with pain. His eye rapidly puffed up like an inflated balloon. It was time to go home and face the music, as El Canalillo had long been declared out of bounds for all of us.

When we arrived, we found a miliciano outside Juanito's flat. The miliciano prevented him from ringing the bell.

'You cannot go in. Nobody can,' he stated in a surly manner.

Juanito removed the hand that was covering his eye. It had now taken yellowish and purple hues. But strangely, there was no blood.

We could hear a man's voice shouting inside. '*Puta!* (whore) I know you're a nun who wants to fool the party. You *hija de puta.*' (whore's daughter). The shouting continued.

The miliciano must have considered the eye condition bad enough to knock on the door repeatedly until a policeman – the person who had been inside shouting – opened it. In low voices, they exchanged words, and we were allowed to go in.

To say that our friend's mother screamed is not enough. Her throat produced such sharp notes as to pierce everybody's eardrums. Mingled with her screams, a woman's sobs could be heard coming from another room.

The policeman tried to calm Juanito's mother.

'How did you get that? Who hit you?', she asked.

No reply.

'What were you doing that you shouldn't have been doing to get that?'

Accusation implied. It did not work. Then, a more charitable approach: 'Does it hurt?'

'No!' A loud no from a tough boy.

The policeman then spoke to Juanito's mother. 'Don't worry unnecessarily. The eye will go back to normal in a few days. Take it from me. I'm an expert because of my occupation... you know... the fist is more effective than words when you need to extract information.'

Every few words, he smiled sardonically with a wry twist of his lips. Nobody had to tell us that there was something nasty going on. The sobbing from inside the other room, possibly the lounge, continued. Fear would have gripped us but for the fact that our skins had been thickened by similar situations.

Juanito's mother, in some kind of stupor, slumped on the edge of a chair. She accepted the policeman's explanation and was now more worried about the fate of the woman who had been so maltreated.

The four of us stayed put around Juanito. Carlota, ever resourceful, nudged me. She had been observing the policeman. Her eyes were trained on his neck. She gave a quick wink, and the rest of us knew the object of her attention. An oversized *nuez* (epiglottis), second only to that of my brother Jesus was moving in a fascinating up-and-down rhythm. The man caught her eye, and she burst into laughter. He gave her an irate look and took a step forward, his hand raised, ready to slap her.

'My father is also a policeman,' she shouted at him stepping back to hide behind me.

He pushed me to one side and got hold of her hair.

'You tell me what you're laughing at or—'

'Your nuez. Your nuez... and... and I'll tell my dad. He's a captain.'

Resourceful Carlota promoted her dad to captain. Well done! In a rage, the policeman let go off her hair. 'Enough of this. Bloody children! Let's get that puta where she belongs.'

He went quickly to the lounge and dragged the sobbing woman to where we were. He shook her repeatedly. 'Stop that pantomime, you fucking bitch.'

A sudden bell ring increased the terror in all of us. Juanito's mother trembling. Juanito hugged her. El Militino still held the bottle with the lizard in it. Carlota and I wished her father could come to take her home.

The door opened. Juanito's father came in, followed by the miliciano. Juanito's father was a serious man. I never saw him smile. His presence projected authority. He calmly surveyed the scene.

'Papers,' roared the Nuez.

Obediently, he placed a wallet in his hand as he pointed to a corner of room, away from the rest of us.

We could only hear the odd word of what was said in that corner, but our intuition told us that the policeman was no longer in command. The Nuez twisted apologetically while Juanito's father, having recovered his wallet, kept on waving it about conveying his annoyance. Now it seemed to be his turn to demand the Nuez's papers. He noted something on a piece of paper.

Another nudge from Carlota. 'He has a pistol.'

Now that the situation had changed, Juanito's mother sighed with relief and took us to the lounge.

'Thank God your dad came just in time.'

'Who's that lady?' asked Juanito.

His mother took a long time to reply. 'Works with… works with your dad.' It was a badly improvised reply, but acceptable.

'Didn't know dad had a pistol.'

She gave no explanation. She just dried her tears.

Juanito's father stayed with the visitors for a long time. His voice rose with words we could hardly understand. The Nuez's voice was also heard, saying, 'Yes, Inspector,' and something that sounded like, 'Sorry, Comrade. Very sorry.'

Eventually, the policeman and miliciano were taken to the door. A loud slam put paid to their visit. Shortly afterwards, we were sent home and Juanito, to bed without dinner.

His father did not chastise him or even enquire as to the cause of his colourful eye, which made us think that he had more important things to worry about.

The sobbing woman had disappeared from the scene double-quick, and the Juanito household went back to normal. He was just as puzzled as the rest of us as to what happened, especially at the discovery of the pistol.

'My dad has also got a pistol, but he's a policeman. My mum has a silver shooter, doesn't she, Manolo?'

'My dad has a revolver.' Clearly, it was time to enumerate who had weapons and to list those weapons. That was my contribution to the list.

El Militino's father did not have those kinds of weapons, but he was not unarmed. 'My dad has a hammer. Nobody is going to mess with him with a hammer in his hand.'

Mystery and Cod Liver Oil

We were sitting at our desk when Juanito appeared the following morning. His eye had completely deflated, as the Nuez had predicted. However, the marks around it had acquired deeper hues of yellow and purple during the night. He received welcoming smiles from the three of us.

A shocked Doña Amalia came to inspect the damage, asking some very original questions. 'What happened to your eye?'

'Nothing,' Juanito replied, as expected.

'Did somebody hit you?'

Shrug.

After drawing such eloquent replies, she returned to her desk. We did not grill Juanito about the events we witnessed, in spite of the curiosity that was tormenting us.

Sometime during the previous evening, I told Maria but she dismissed it as a fib. I also told Rafael. He was more receptive. 'These *mierdas*. If they find anything suspicious, they will use any method to get the truth out of people. Perhaps that woman is a friend of the Nationals. Perhaps…' He decided not to continue.

'But Juanito's father carries a pistol.'

'Now, that's not unusual.'

I could sense that there was something he did not want to say. I had observed a similar attitude in other grown-ups when they did not want children to know certain things.

Carlota had her own ideas. She told me on our way to school. 'I think Juanito's father must be a policeman. You saw the way he shut the Nuez up. A boss in the force.'

'And the woman?'

'A secret agent. I'm sure. You heard him say, "Sorry, Comrade".'

I liked Carlota's logic. Always on target. Surely she must have learnt that from her father.

Before school ended, Mari Paz stood on the plinth by her mother's desk and made an announcement.

'We have been fortunate to get a few bottles of cod liver oil for you all. Cod liver oil is wonderful to build up your strength. Now that food is scarce, it will be a great help for your health. So after chanting the tables and capitals of the world, I'd like you to line up and come here.'

The only thing missing from her eloquent announcement was that 'cod liver oil cures all ills'.

El Militino reservedly expressed his instant dislike to the idea. 'It's '☐☐orrible,' he said in a low voice, but it was loud enough to be heard.

'It's not that bad. You'll be having one spoon each.'

'My mum gives it to me when I'm banged up.'

Mari Paz thought quickly. 'I'm sure what your mum gives you is not cod liver oil,' she said in a pacifying voice.

'Yes. It's an "orrible" oil.'

'Won't it be castor oil you're thinking about?' We took on board the idea of castor oil. We had experienced its taste and rapid effects. Perhaps El Militino's gut owed its capricious modus operandi to that kind of lubrication. 'And after taking the cod liver oil, you can have a lick at half a lemon that I have got ready to make things more palatable,' Mari Paz added.

With our chanting over, Doña Amalia, the true holder of the fortifying oil, donned an apron to shield any spillages that could contaminate her clothes. Then, spoon in hand, she was ready to administer the oil. Mari Paz, holding a lemon cut in half, was at her side smiling benignly as the proceedings started. We were each given a spoon of the oil and a lick at lemon until all of us had our share. Licking the lemon as a palate refresher and taking some of the dribble belonging to the preceding licker would now be frowned upon as a potential source of infection. But in those days, that kind of silly trivia did not enter our minds, and nobody I know caught the dreaded lurgy in the process.

A few days later, I overheard Pepe and Rafael talking about a purge. A word that so far, I'd only associated with something medicinal to clear your intestines. But they used it with a different meaning. The snippets of conversation helped me understand that there were some of us secretly smuggling people out of the Red Zone in order to save their lives.

My brothers talked about newspapers publishing stories of individuals who worked for the enemies of the Party and supported the obscurantist ideas of the Church, wanting nothing but death for them. I boiled all that down to one sentence: Those helping priests and nuns could expect nothing but death.

I was sure Juanito's father was engaged in saving people from the clutches of the Reds. His staunch Catholic faith was an indicator for that, as the whole family as well as my mother and Maria regularly congregated in their flat to say the rosary and pray for the restoration of peace – an activity which would have cost all concerned dearly. This suspicion of mine was also reinforced by Juanito's complete silence.

At Death's Door

Maria was not the only one to go down with an intestinal infection. I also suffered that trouble. One day, quite unexpectedly, about two hours after the midday meal, my belly was assaulted by terrible pain accompanied by liquid diarrhoea and a high fever. My legs would not hold me and after being put to bed by my sister Martina, I experienced more excruciating pain. I was thirsty like I had never been before. A doctor from the Red Cross came to see me. Physically he was nothing like Doctor Don Juan Bonachera.

After so many years, I can still recall his image. Small. Thin as a rake. Bones protruding despite the padded shoulders of his jacket. A garden brush moustache impeding the air to his nose. But the most remarkable of his characteristics was an intermittent tapping of the end of the stem of his reading glasses on one of his eyes, making a tap-tapping sound. Later Martina revealed that he had a glass eye.

My temperature was taken and then my belly felt with icy cold fingers. Then a plan of attack: No food. Plenty of mineral water if it could be found plus a huge bottle of a saline solution readily brought in by a nurse from the same stable.

The words 'dehydration' and 'gastroenteritis' were bandied about amongst members of my family, quick to learn medical jargon. Gastroenteritis – the inflammation of the colon and small intestine. It was no joke, especially when the retortijones (rapid twists of the intestinal tract) screwed my guts. Then the pain was so incredible that I even stopped breathing.

In the absence of mineral water, glasses of water from the tap that originated from the Lozoya canal and the injecting of the saline solution transformed my anatomy from severe drought into a properly irrigated field. After a few days of starvation, Doctor Glass Eye decreed a diet of grated apple and carrot puree. Mash potatoes would follow.

Carlota came to see me, and somehow she managed to get through my mother's defences.

It was like this: In the absence of a working bell, Carlota knocked on the door time and time again until my mother opened it.

'I'm Carlota… from upstairs.'

Silence from my mother, who eyed the immobile urchin.

'My father is a policeman… and my mother has given me something for Manolo.'

I am sure my mother was itching to send 'the devil's daughter' away with distaste. But she still said nothing.

'Tio Morales told me…

'Senor Morales, child, senor Morales,' scolded my mother.

'Yes. Yes. Doña Maria Antonia, Senor Morales says Manolo is not well. He saw the doctor and then he also saw the nurse.'

'So?'

'I'd like to see Manolo, Doña Maria Antonia, please.' As she was saying that, she offered my mother a small parcel that she had been hiding behind her back. 'This is for Manolo, for Manolo when he is better.'

The ice started to melt. A little smile emerged. Also the appearance of Michito helped.

'You'd better come in.'

The little parcel contained two square ounces of chocolate, her customary companion.

My friend was taken to the lounge, where my friend was acquainted with my condition and there was a preliminary chat between Saint Antonio de Padua's protégé and 'Red' Carlota.

Several times during my convalescence she was allowed in to see me, but she spent more time with my mother than with me. In a few days, they took to each other like long-lost friends.

Once I heard my mother say to my father, 'She's such a lovely child. So clever for somebody of that young age.'

A miracle!

So the 'lovely child' suggested that Juanito and El Militino could also come to see me now that I was a little better. My mother considered it. Juanito, because of his inventions, was a danger to himself and to others. As for El Militino and his capriciousness, well. It was a no, no, to both.

But Carlota kept the fires of friendship amongst the four of us burning. A few days later I overheard 'Manolo's friends asked me to bring this box. Hope it'll be all right, Doña Maria Antonia.' She deposited the box, a shoebox, on the kitchen table. It had a few holes in the lid.

'There are two silk worms in it.'

The lid was lifted and the two inhabitants, fat and wriggly were peacefully eating a mulberry leaf.

'The worms are from El Militino; Juanito gets the mulberry leaves from the small house in Principe de Vergara. The box is from my mother's shoes. I painted it and made the holes in the lid.'

My mother was pleased and rewarded Carlota by allowing her to put La Chugue to swim. The kitchen sink was filled with water; the washboard placed on one of the narrow sides like a ramp; and La Chugue slid down it and into the water.

My mother remained in the kitchen with my friend, peeling a few potatoes, which had seen better days or, in Shakespeare speak, passed their first freshness. The potatoes were a donation from an unknown benefactor, who preferred to remain anonymous by leaving them outside our flat door.

The stock of mulberry leaves was almost extinct. Carlota undertook to replenish it. Here is how she did it. Like Juanito she went to the small house, so called because of its size as compared with the eight-story-high blocks that surrounded it. The gate was closed. After ringing the bell several times and getting no reply, she decided to scale the fence to get into the garden. The mulberry tree was surrounded by a circular bench, on which she stood to reach the branches. She had hardly finished collecting some leaves when the barking of a dog startled her. The barking preceded the appearance of a small canine in full flight.

There was only one thing to do. Run and run fast.

The fence was only a few feet away from the tree. There was no time to even think. Fear propelled her over the top and into the street.

Fuelled by adrenaline, she continued to run most of the way and chose to deliver the supplies before returning home. She proudly delivered the loot to a reception committee formed by my mother, Michito, and myself already over the belly crisis.

Carlota looked excited. Almost as excited as when her mother's shooter went off. I noticed her knee was bleeding. So did my mother.

'What's happened to your knee?' she asked

Shrug.

'Did you fall?'

One more shrug.

'You must have done.'

'Dunno.'

I suspected something had happened, something she did not want to tell. While the miraculous oxygenated water was being fetched, she told me.

'There was this stupid dog chasing me, barking like an idiot. At first I thought it was a big dog. I was scared, but when I was in the street, I saw it was a stupid little mongrel.'

At my mother's return, Carlotta stopped speaking. Her knee was profusely dabbed. A few minutes later she was despatched home but not before she managed to finish her confession.

'So I kicked it, but my foot went through the railings and the mongrel grabbed hold of my shoe. I had to pull real hard to get my foot back and scratched my knee.'

I felt proud to have such a brave friend and vowed to relate her bravery blow-by-blow to Juanito and El Militino as soon as I was allowed out.

The Dead Man

During a pause in the lessons, Carlota had something to tell us. 'My mum says that Rosie the cow has had two little calves and that we can go and see them after school.' Rosie was one of the residents of *La Vaqueria* (the cow house) in Principe de Vergara. It was a great idea, and we voted unanimously to do so.

The cod liver oil and lemon licking was improved at Larrumbe by adding a Vienna roll. So, fortified in this way, the four of us made our way to La Vaqueria, up General Oraa, making a right turn on the corner of the Augustines Church, where the body of brother Ruperto had been found. We always tried to avoid that corner, but on this occasion, due to the situation of La Vaqueria, we could not.

Principe de Vergara was an unusual place to keep twelve cows of the finest Swiss pedigree, in the middle of Madrid and only a stone's throw from where we lived. Such a place would now not just be frowned upon but considered simply unthinkable because of hygiene and animal rights in mind.

The vaqueria was a long nave with open bays facing a white wall instead of the alfalfa fields. Above each bay, the name of the resident was painted in red: Rosie, Margarita, Emerald, and so on. The bays were big enough for the animals to stand. No room for moving about. A ditch ran along the opposite side all the length of the nave, irrigated by an intermittent flow of water, to take care of waste products. A square glass window overlooking the street allowed the daylight in and passers-by to observe the herd. Next to the square window, a folding metal door enabled the herd to come out for the necessary daily constitution. That part of Principe de Vergara was gifted with the sight and smell of nature.

We were given a conducted tour by a vaquero. 'Don't they get bored looking at the wall all the time?' El Militino asked, concerned about their welfare.

'They get used to it. Cows don't like too much moving about. I take them for a stroll every day. That's all they want.' The vaquero sounded convincing.

We knew about their strolls, as the cows seemed compelled to relieve themselves, splashing the evidence on the asphalt the minute they came out into the street. We also knew that these cows supplied Senor Brigido with the milk we drank.

Our visit to the vaqueria afforded us a view of the calves, which according to Carlota, were the colour of cinnamon, whilst Juanito settled for a more prosaic light brown. We spent a while admiring the new comers and wondering where they would be kept when they grew bigger. We asked the vaquero.

'When they are a little bigger, we'll send them to the farm. We always do that with the calves. If you come back a little later you can see the cows being milked.'

We exchanged looks. Yes. We would do that.

'Perhaps when you are a little bigger, you could help with the milking.' This was an invitation extended exclusively to Carlota, who promised to ruminate about it. That concluded episode one of our visit. Time now for us to move to new pastures.

'We can go get some mulberry leaves,' suggested Juanito.

The small house was on the opposite side; it was only a matter of crossing the road.

'That mongrel is still there,' announced Carlota.

'Is it the one who bit your shoe?' El Militino remembered the incident.

'He's not barking this time,' I said.

The so-baptised mongrel was a little dog, perhaps a Bichon Frise. It seemed to be distressed –it was whining and not barking. It came to the gate and stood by it, whining all the time. We rang the bell several times and waited, but nobody answered.

'The gate is not locked.' Juanito took action, and we went in. The dog seemed to welcome that. He started towards the entrance to the house and waited for us to follow.

'Strange. He was such a nuisance last time, and look at him now, so nice.'

The door to the house was ajar. Another bell to ring. Again, no answer.

The dog stopped with us by the door. His whining more intense, and he let out an occasional yelp.

Carlota picked him up. 'What's the matter? What's the matter, Pippo?'

'Pippo? Do you know his name?' we asked.

She gave a sad smile as she felt the dog was in a sorry state. 'It's written on his collar.'

Our mood, which so far had been a happy one, changed swiftly as if something adverse was about to happen.

'If he could talk, he'd tell us why he's so distressed,' El Militino said.

'He doesn't need to talk. He's already shown us he's not very happy.' Then Juanito pushed the door open a fraction and called, 'Hello?'

We joined in. He gave another small push to the door, and it opened wide. Pippo struggled to free himself from Carlota's arms.

'He's shaking like a leaf,' she said, letting him go. Yelping, he made towards the gate, where he stopped.

We followed Juanito into the house. It appeared to be empty and there was a smell of rot in the air. Stealthily, we opened a few doors that led to empty rooms.

'I think we ought to go,' I suggested. That said, I still followed Juanito and the others, this time into the lounge. We were guided by a strange smell like that of putrid meat.

Pippo came back to the entrance door and stopped there.

Once in the lounge, horror struck us. The body of a man lay head down along the length of a large sofa. An arm hung towards the floor. His back was covered in coagulated blood.

'Quick. Let's get out!' Juanito made for the door. We followed.

'We must tell somebody,' I said.

'Tell your dad, Carlota. He's a policeman.' El Militino chose the right person.

On the way out, Carlota picked up Pippo. 'You're coming with us,' she reassured him.

We made our way home half walking, half running, without giving a thought to the milking in La Vaqueria.

When Carlota's mother answered the door and was faced with the four of us and a little dog, she was not quite sure what to expect. We were too perturbed to speak coherently, especially when the four of us spoke at the same time. But little by little, we unburdened ourselves.

Later, I learned that Pippo had been entrusted to one of Carlota's aunts and that her father had been detailed to investigate the matter. We never knew any more about the dead man or why he was murdered. But considering he was a wealthy man with right-wing ideas, and as such, it is not too difficult to assume that his murder was put down to the turmoil of the Civil War.

Uncle Pepe

But for a little maize bread, hard and strange to the palate, my sister Maria and I had no food. And no food the day before. We were totally destitute. We did not feel hungry anymore. Even hunger had disowned us long ago. As a sign of rebellion against the inbuilt need to eat, a dead feeling of emptiness had replaced the pangs of appetite. It was an uncanny protest against the lack of food.

We were thin. Almost skeletal. And weak. But what troubled us most was the cold. The flat where we lived, the flat where we were born, once elegant and cosy, presented now the stamp of desolation. Most of the wooden furniture had gone, used as fuel in the kitchen range, burnt in an attempt to bring the temperature above freezing. Wooden shutters, chairs, and tables were sacrificed to the fire. There was nowhere to sit but for a few upside-down metal buckets, originally designated for coal, which was now impossible to obtain.

My bigger brothers stole two tubular trestles and a metal sheet from somewhere to make a table. We put it in the dining room in the hope that one day we might be able to sit round it like we used to, when the sun shone through our balconies and the aroma of coffee roasting in the street below, outside the grocer's store filled the air – in the days before tragedy struck.

My mother in a desperate effort to get some food into our famished bodies sent us to see Auntie Nativity. She lived far away, one hour's walk, at least. Maria was lucky; she had shoes, a pair that someone had given her. They were too big for her feet, but after stuffing a ball of paper into the toes, fitted 'as good as made to measure', according to my mother.

I had no shoes other than an improvised pair of sandals, if one could call them that, made from discarded tyres tied with string. It was anybody's guess whether they could take me to Auntie Nativity and back. We had no socks. The freezing cold and wet pavements made us aware of that.

We did not really want to go and see Auntie Nativity, kind as she was, since cousin Daniel, whom we saw frequently, was not there anymore. Also, there was Uncle Pepe to consider. Lately he had turned surly and abrupt, always looking miserable and making us feel unwanted. Sometimes I thought he was right. Who was going to want us? Who was going to want my mother and rest of my brothers and sisters, ten of us in all, now that we had nothing? Now that the war had taken all we had.

'Uncle Pepe is not so bad,' my mother told me.

Maria knew why he did not want us, but she did not want to talk about it. It was clear she was hiding something. I could tell by the way she averted her eyes. I knew the real reason why he was now the way he was. But I would not tell, either.

At midday we set off for Auntie Nativity's home. There were no kisses, no hugs from mother. As things were, we did not show affection or get emotional or too attached to each other. This was an unwritten rule, to minimise suffering when it came. And if the future was anything like the past had been and like the present was, more suffering was bound to come. We all seemed to know that tragedy could strike at any time, as it had already done so many times.

We walked down Velazquez Boulevard, which was lined with acacia trees. On either side ran the tram rails and overhead cables that provided the electricity that made the trams go. That day they were running more slowly than usual. There was very little power on the line, and they crawled along, clanking and chattering their metal words as they passed, whining submissively.

A ride cost money. Money that we did not have. It was very cold. Our fingers were numb. Our ears ached. I took the precaution of lining my sweater with folded newspapers to combat the cold. In spite of that, I could feel goose pimples on my skin.

My coat was in tatters, thinned with time, a pitiful scrap of cloth for Madrid's savage winter. We walked fast, shivering. Our teeth chattered, but we did not acknowledge the cold. We must not feel the cold. Another unwritten rule for survival.

The thought of not reaching our destination did not enter our heads. We would not let it. We talked little in order to conserve energy and to prevent the cold air from entering our lungs. If it did, we would cough like my eldest brother, who was down with consumption. We were told the cold air gave him a strange wheezing cough, a persistent cough that scared me.

My feet were purple and nearly frozen. But not all was bad. The aeroplanes had not come that day. Not yet, anyhow. They would come later, at night, and the sirens would roar their raspy warning. Then the bombs would fall. Like they had the night before. Like they did time and time again. But now the sirens were silent – so far.

At the end of the boulevard, we turned into Alcala Street, a main artery leading to the centre of Madrid. We passed Retiro Park, Alcala's Gate, and the main post office, where we turned into El Prado Walk, then the small streets, and finally Las Huertas, where Auntie Nativity lived.

She was not surprised at the state we were in. She embraced us warmly. 'You're so cold!'

'No… No, Auntie… We are not…'

We had been taught to deny our own feelings. I do not understand why this should be so. Maria, in spite of being older than me, did not know either. We could hardly speak. It was difficult when our lips were cracking and our jaws could hardly move.

Auntie Nativity managed to get fresh sardines in the black market. She fried six at a time in a large frying pan. The oil splattered. At the smell of frying fish, a lost memory of the tasty swimmers came back.

We were sitting in the kitchen. When the first batch was ready, we started to eat, and as we did so, the hunger that had been dormant for days, awakened and we ate fast, almost to the point of choking.

'Milk, have some milk to help it go down,' Auntie said. She appeared nervous. I did not think she wanted Uncle Pepe to see us.

Maria spoke in a whisper, 'Quick, before he comes. He must not catch us eating. Won't like that. He's peculiar.' I chose not to hear what she said.

There was a knock on the door. It was him! Now we all felt nervous, a strange feeling that we shared without words.

Soon he was in the kitchen with us. His hair was white, and his hands were bluish with cold. On his face was a look of pity. I could recognise this look. I had seen it so many times when people looked at me. But Uncle Pepe's expression was somewhat different. His face showed the defeat of the helpless. The desperation of being powerless.

For a time he did not say anything. He just sat with us quietly. Out of the corner of my eye, I could see that Auntie Nativity was crying silently, trying to disguise her tears.

Uncle Pepe took a small bundle from his jacket pocket and unwrapped it carefully: two magdalenas. He gave one to Maria and one to me. When the time came for us to go, he took his scarf off and put it round my neck. He was not wearing a shirt or a sweater. He did not possess one, only a vest under his jacket, a dark brown corduroy jacket that had seen better times.

'It'll keep the cold away,' he said, then he pressed some coins into my hand. 'For the tram, Manolo.'

His voice warmed as he spoke. He looked sad, sad like Auntie Nativity, but his eyes did not shine.

Maria told me that men do not cry. Much later, when I was bigger I would, perhaps, tell her that men also cry. When they are alone.

Uncle Pepe looked at me with sadness. His eyes delivered an unspoken message: cousin Daniel was not with us anymore.

Aladdin's Lamp

Money was scarce. All avenues to save it were explored. Somebody must have discovered a way of stopping the electric meter from running. Juanito, his mind spurred by pure logic and a keen dollop of observation, became wise to the trick.

'I know how it's done, Manolo.' He paused to produce the desired effect and whet my curiosity. 'Our meter is by the entrance door.'

'That's where all the meters are.'

'I've seen my dad putting something in it. If somebody rings the bell, he pulls it out until the person goes. Then he puts it back. Why do you think he does that?'

'Dunno.'

'I do. Heard him telling my mum: no more high bills from those robbers at the electricity company.'

This was truly simple! A thin metal ribbon, often originating from an old pocket watch or a wind-up toy mechanism was inserted through a gap at the bottom of the meter and pushed in until it made contact with the turning disc that registered the units used.

I fathomed out that this was a clandestine operation and nobody should know about it. After this revelation, I kept my eye on our meter. When my father was in, a thin bit stuck out of the bottom of the meter, and as Juanito said, when somebody knocked on the door, he pulled it out and into his pocket it went.

This method became so widely known that the electricity company brought in a modification. If the disc stopped running, the fuses melted. Power cuts became lengthier as the war went on. Many times there was no current for hours on end, and we had to resort to a *quinque* (paraffin lamp) for lighting. In the quinque, which was made entirely of glass with a fascinating long tube to shield the flame, a wick rested in the paraffin deposit. Its light mitigated the darkness and created a dreamy atmosphere that I liked; I felt happy under its glow.

To supplement the quinque, the *candil* (oil lamp) came into play. The candil was an all-metal gadget with a shallow base where wick and oil resided. Its use was relegated to the kitchen, where it hung from a nail on the wall opposite the range and gave out light of dubious value. According to my mother, it emanated a noxious pong and more smoke than light, depending on the oil used and the stuff the wick was made with. Maria favoured the theory that it must have been made from tufts around Satan's hooves.

The whole family were in agreement with mother, who felt darkness was better than the consequences of being subjected to the awful effects of the candil. Michito did not mind the darkness, and on those occasions when fish oil was used, he seemed to enter a special paradise all of his own.

Not all is doom and gloom in adverse conditions. One day my father brought home a headlight from a veteran car – it was a beautiful lamp, worthy of Aladdin.

The whole family gathered round the dining room table to hear how it worked.

'Pity there's no genie,' I could not help exclaiming.

My father smiled. 'But there's one. It is hidden here,' he said, producing a chalky lump. 'This is *carburo*. In contact with water, it gives out a gas, and when you put a match to it burns with a very bright flame.'

My bigger brothers understood. I was still waiting to see the genie.

'The genie, Manolo, is the gas that gives the light.'

I must have looked disappointed.

'What better to ask the lamp for than light?'

I had to agree. A genie giving us light! Wow!

The lamp was made of shiny metal and bevelled glass with two chambers, one above the other. The carburo, calcium carbide, was destined for the lower chamber, water, for the upper one. A small valve allowed the water to drip onto the carburo. That released the gas

'Then the genie is out, Manolo. Put a match to it, and he will appear disguised as a bright flame,' my father concluded, all excited.

This was definitely very important news to share with Juanito. He was mesmerised by the idea. 'I know what we can do to have a flame of our own.' For such an important venture, Carlota and El Militino were summoned.

I 'borrowed' a lump of carburo and the four of us, arms resting on each other's shoulders and singing, went to El Canalillo to carry out another one of Juanito's experiments.

El Militino contributed an empty can of pilchards redolent with the aroma of the fish, still pungent, even in the free atmosphere of the open fields. The can had a small hole at the unopened end, artistically made by El Militino. Carlota brought a box with a few matches in it. Some looked as if expecting them to light would be futile.

Juanito, in charge of the proceedings, allocated the jobs. I would make a hole just big enough for the can to fit tightly in and drop the carburo into it. El Militino would fill any gaps around it. Juanito reserved for himself the pouring of the water, which he had brought in a hip flask, through the hole.

Carlota, in full Raven regalia – red cotton cloth covering her hair, black eye mask, though regrettably the shiny shooter had been replaced by the box of soggy matches – was chosen for the top job of igniting the gas. Unfortunately, match after match failed to work. We could hear the hissing of the gas inside the can. Disappointment was setting in. Then, suddenly, there was a bang and the can took to the air.

Juanito, never lost for words, announced, 'We have created a rocket.'

'Much better than setting fire to the gas.' Carlota was in full support.

'A can without the hole in the top would be much better.' A bright idea from El Militino.

'The rocket would fly much higher,' I added.

A bright future in the rocket business was awaiting us.

When I returned home I found Uncle Fabian talking to my mother. It was bad news. He had been summoned to appear before some committee. A depurating committee, according to Maria. His back had healed at long last, but he still refrained from picking me up as he used to. That made me think he was not completely recovered.

The Committee

Uncle Fabian, with characteristic aplomb, informed Fulgencio of the peremptory summons he received to appear before the Depurating Committee. Although Fulgencio, as Responsable, had to be seen as enforcer of the communistic ruling, he had become too friendly with my father and uncles for his own good. Also, after months in his official post of Responsable, the seeds of power had gone to his head, inflating his zest for authority. Montero Hermanos was his domain, and nobody but nobody was going to interfere with those under his watch.

'What's all this about, Comrade?' His demeanour stamped a rictus of protection on his countenance.

Uncle Fabian related the episode of the cat when the curfew was about to start.

'I know that hijo de puta. That's el cabron who patrols this neighbourhood.'

We never knew his name, but for all intents and purposes, baptising him El Cabron fitted the bill admirably. Uncle Fabian also mentioned that el hijo de puta told him about a pending summons with the Depurating Committee. Fulgencio's face turned purple. 'That's all the doing of that cabron. He deserves una patada en los cojones, and one of these days I'm going to administer it myself.'

His words seem to dissipate his anger to a certain extent. Then he added in a low voice, 'These are troubled times. It's difficult to trust anybody. We don't know who our friends or enemies are.' He exhaled deeply. It was an obvious sign of the idealist within him! Then in an even lower voice, he said, 'Tell me, is there anything you have to hide?'

An expected question. 'Myself and my three brothers were in service for many years until the Duke financed Salvador…'

'Comrade Salvador,' corrected Fulgencio with inequitable pride.

'Being in service meant that we worked our days and nights to the bone. We were workers, and we knew who the oppressors were.' A touch of inspiration!

'But the Duke was generous.'

'The Duke, I'm sure, was a socialist in disguise.' Another touch of inspiration by my uncle – even better!

A few moments passed for Fulgencio to digest what was said. 'I'll come with you to the committee, and they're going to hear me, brother.'

It was a very great honour, and to be called 'brother' to boot! My father soon got to know of Fulgencio's intention to accompany my uncle. Siding up with somebody in his charge could have detrimental consequences for El Responsable.

'Comrade Fulgencio, Fabian is grateful for your help. But it worries me that your appearance at the tribunal could be detrimental for a man in your position. They may think you're a turncoat. Only… the devil knows that.' My father took great effort to replace God with the devil, as the current climate required. 'My brother has never been mixed up in behaving against the authorities. By nature he's a worker, through and through.'

A worker through and through! This was music to El Responsable's ears. Fulgencio assented, but nothing was going to change his mind. Also, he had an account to settle with El Cabron, and this was a golden opportunity for revenge.

The Depurating Committee was a milder form of persecution as compared with the cheka. In the former, severe, often brutal, methods of interrogation were used. In the cheka, death was usually the end result.

On the appointed day, Fulgencio loaded my uncle in the sidecar of his motorcycle and delivered him to the Committee. Taking a suspect of subversive activities on an official motorcycle was only done in extraordinary circumstances. That alone was bad enough, but when he entered the designated room announcing to the Tribunal that a horrendous error had been committed with one of his workers, an unfortunate situation of his own creation exploded – shouts and threats amidst a turbulent competition of who could blaspheme the loudest. Eventually the persuasive entrance of several milicianos with rifles at the ready restored silence.

El Responsable, in the heat of his fiery temper, accused El Cabron of having engineered false accusation against Comrade Fabian, who was no more than a simpleton and a tireless worker. My uncle was unceremoniously pushed into one of the dreaded interrogation rooms.

In the early hours of the morning, a car stopped outside the flat where my uncle lived with my auntie Efigenia and cousins Angel and Alfonso, one year older than me, and a true accomplice in our infantile exploits. Four agents of the Secret Brigade alighted from the car and trampled to the third floor, their hobnailed boots sparking on the stone staircase. Then came the sinister thumping of their fists against the wooden door.

Auntie Efigenia, renowned for her sharp tongue, answered the door armed with the thin kitchen range poker.

'What have you done with my husband?' she hollered, lifting the poker.

In reply, she got a clout across her face. 'Where's the gun?' the threatening voice of the leader demanded.

Auntie Efigenia had been so worried about my uncle that she was unable to sleep. In a fit of anger, she indiscriminately attacked the four agents, kicking, screaming, and biting, without much success. The agents, as if they were in the presence of a wild animal, punched her to the ground, where she remained unconscious. The flat was searched. No gun was found. My cousins were terrified at witnessing such barbarous conduct.

Cousin Alfonso wasted no time in relating what happened. I could see how scared he was at the thought that something like this could happen again. Neither him nor Angel and my auntie knew the fate of Uncle Fabian. Luckily, Auntie Efigenia recovered quickly.

Uncle Fabian's name was only mentioned at home under a shroud of sadness. Even Maria did not know what might have happened. We felt he would never again be with us; no doubt he had been killed by the Red assassins. The thought of Brother Ruperto transfixed to a tree with a bayonet in his belly came back to haunt me, day and night, day and night.

The existence of snipers was a normal consequence of the civil war. I remember hearing single shots that intermittently broke the silence of the night. Maria used to call them pakkos because of the noise they made. Pak-ko! The bullets were not directed at a particular target; they were simply a helpless expression of protest.

A long time after the war finished, my cousin Pedro confessed that he'd been one of them. He told me he still possessed a black nine-millimetre pistol that, through force of habit, he always kept with him.

Contrary to what Maria and I thought, Uncle Fabian had not been killed by the Reds. I did not see him for a long time, and when I did I could but notice deep scars on either side of his mouth. He hugged me. A long-lasting hug that made me feel his tears trickling down my face. He spoke little then. He waited until I was much older and capable of understanding what went on with the Depurating Committee. El Cabron had falsely accused him of possessing a gun and being a sniper. During the period of interrogation, he was hit with a brick across the face.

'They couldn't break me, Manolo. They couldn't break me. Now all that is in the past.'

There were no adverse consequences for the actions of El Responsable at the Committee. He was obviously well anchored within the Party. We never discovered the 'account' he had to settle with El Cabron.

After so many years, I can still hear El Cabron's voice as he patrolled our streets at night to make sure the curfew was obeyed and all lights were out, *'Esas luces'* (those lights), commanding complete darkness to avoid being spotted by enemy planes.

Shortly after the detention of Uncle Fabian, a different voice shouted 'Esas luces' at night, which made the grown-ups in my family wonder if Fulgencio had in fact settled his account with El Cabron.

Maximo

With the disappearance of Uncle Fabian, cousin Alfonso stayed with us. That kept his spirits up somewhat. To entertain us, my mother used to tell us stories, actual events of when she was a child herself. We sat round the dining room table because there was no such a thing as a lounge at home. Putting on a special voice, which could range from mysterious to excited, she announced, 'I'm going to tell you the story of Maximo.'

'Who was Maximo, Auntie Maria Antonia?' asked Alfonso, full of curiosity.

'You'll know if you listen to the story.' We crossed our arms in anticipation.

'When I was a little girl—'

'Did you have yellow hair like Carmina?'

'No. My hair was black. Long, to my waist. When I was a little girl,' she continued, 'I lived in Yunquera de Henares, a small village in the Guadalajara province, not far from Madrid. There, with my older sister Nativity, I often got into trouble for all manner of tricks.'

'Nativity is my Auntie Nati,' I explained to Alfonso.

'We liked to go down to the railway station to see the trains. Uncle Patricio often travelled to the capital. On his return we would be at the station to greet him. Do you remember Uncle Patricio, Manolo?'

I did remember him, as a tall, straight man with strong features and a ramrod back.

'He always brought us a treat.' My mother closed her eyes for a second as if to reminisce.

'A treat?' I was curious to know.

'Something nice. But one day he announced the best treat it of all. We would go to Guadalajara with him to buy stuff for the Virgen de la Granja fair. La Virgen de la Granja was found hidden under a blackberry bush by little children many years ago. The people of Yunquera made her a chapel, where she has resided ever since. Every year on the fifteenth of September, the Virgin is paraded through the village, and so commence the festivities, which last for two weeks. There are celebrations for all to enjoy. La Plaza Mayor (the village square), opposite the Town Hall, is adorned with bunting; banners, and other outdoor decorations, such as garlands of local flowers festooning the acacia trees that surround the square. There are stalls selling frosted fruits and tasty morsels to eat, trinkets, and curio.'

'What's curio?' we asked.

'Curio is short for curiosity items,' my mother explained. 'In the evenings a ball, music, and attractions like jugglers and puppet shows take place. But the most important attraction is the melon-growing competition, which gives large prizes for the biggest ones. Uncle Patricio always took part and never won. Always came in second to Old Martin, a nasty man, who makes fun of Uncle in the most cruel way.'

'What was the first prize?' asked Alfonso.

'A medal of la Virgen de la Granja and five duros.'

Five duros. A lot of money!'

'Did a lot of people put their melons in?'

'Several growers entered the competition, but none of them could match the quality of Uncle's and Old Martin's,' my mother replied. 'The day of the journey came and my mum – that was Granny Martina, Manolo – dressed us in new clothes and straw hats with a red ribbon around the brim. We rode to the station with Uncle Patricio in his cart on an unmade path full of potholes that rocked the cart and us within it.

'The platform was crowded. The train, more so. Nati, moving like a squirrel in a hurry, managed to get a seat by the window, where we joined her with the help of other passengers. It was a tight squeeze sitting in an already full compartment, smoky and full, with the smell of dark tobacco. It was hot in the September sun, which made everybody perspire.

'There was a lot of activity. Peddlers selling *peladillas* (sugared almonds) of different colours, white, pink, green even pale blue ones, and *almendras garrapinadas*, a kind of honey-covered crunchy delight in a nice tall carton that Nati and I could not resist and ate till the last one was gone. Entertainers too paraded through, making the time pass quickly. A bronzed man playing the flute became a fixture close to us, much to everybody's delight. Another was selling raffle tickets at a cent each to win a papier-mâché bull.'

A faraway explosion made my mother pause. We sat unmoved. No comments. No sign of fear. Just the determination to ignore the horrors of the war.

'Food was part of the fun,' my mother continued. 'Baskets with food, leather bottles with wine, large round loaves of tasty bread, and round aluminium containers with potato omelettes appeared from the travellers' own luggage, in keeping with tradition.

'Soon everybody was eating with great gusto. Food circulated from person to person in a happy exchange. Red wine, from a leather bottle belonging to a man who was vermilion in the face with heat and drink, did the rounds. Great fun was had by all. Uncle Patricio laughed heartily. Black smoke laced with whitish steam and the occasional whistle burst accompanied us to our destination.'

We were mesmerised by my mother's tale, although the big words she sometimes used went over our heads. I could imagine the train ploughing through the scorched fields, kilometre after kilometre. Villages, small dots in the distance, went by in a circular motion, as if the train was stopped.

'I was on a train before...' Alfonso halted. 'With my father...', His tears did not allow him to continue.

My mother moved her chair closer to his and, resting her arm on his shoulders, said, 'You'll soon know about Maximo. After a day in Guadalajara, getting stuff for the fair, we returned to Yunquera. The following day we rode on Rucio, Uncle Patricio's donkey, to the orchard. We felt sad that Uncle Patricio had never won first prize in the competition. It was the dream of his life! We spent the morning collecting the ripe melons. Then we loaded them in Rucio's panniers.

'Old Martin's field was adjacent, so a visit to him was indicated. We found him sitting on the ground, rifle across his lap, outside his bull rusher's hut, with a big mastiff dog lying next to him.'

'A mastiff!' exclaimed Alfonso. 'Did he bite?'

'Not in the slightest. Nati, your auntie Nativity, used to put her hand to his mouth and he licked it as a sign of affection,' my mother said. Then she went on, '"You've come with those two urchins to spy on my melons, haven't you?" he taunted. "You'll never win first prize as long as I'm alive."

'No answer. Old Martin was given to become grumpy if contradicted, and Uncle would rather not be the target of his bad temper. He wished he could win first prize, if only to show Old Martin that he was not unbeatable. But no matter how hard he tried, he had never succeeded.

'"Your seed is inferior. Planting all wrong. Bad watering. How can you expect to grow good melons? You'll never win as long as I'm alive." Old Martin always behaved like that when the time of the fair approached. Perhaps he did that to undermine his rival's spirits. Uncle Patricio, although hurt, kept silent.

'But old Martin also had an amiable side. it was not all nastiness. After blasting his barrage, he stood up with some difficulty and showed us around his orchard. He bent over a plant whose stems extended over several feet and, pulling some of the covering leaves apart, said, "This is Maximo, the fellow who's going to win this year's first prize. Look at it. Nobody but nobody can grow a larger melon. Look at it well. The colour of a toad's skin. Green and beautiful. I'm not letting your uncle see it. He'll never survive the shock!" Maximo was truly a great specimen to be proud of.

'The air was hot and stifling under a clear blue sky. Old Martin swept the perspiration across his tanned face with the back of his hand. He cast a sinister look. Then, in a conspiratorial voice he said, "You may be asking yourselves why I have my rifle with me, aren't you? To shoot trespassers dead is the answer. They don't come back when they're dead, do they?" He accompanied his words with an intermittent cough that made his body shudder. 'We walked away from him as soon as we could. Back to Uncle and Rucio.'

'Uncle Patricio has no chance against Maximo,' I said, anticipating defeat.

'I don't like Old Martin. He didn't have to say nasty things about Uncle Patricio. He's rotten nasty. He is! Doesn't deserve to win', Nati expressed her feelings.

'The aroma of ripe melons pervaded the air, an aroma that conveyed a feeling of sweetness. "This is the one thing Old Martin's melons don't have," Uncle Patricio said, "Aroma! They also lack sweetness. Mine taste of honey. But the judges don't care about those things. All they are interested in is size, even if they have no taste. My melons are of superior quality but smaller. This is why I'll never win,"

'On the way back walking beside Rucio, we enjoyed the fragrance coming from the panniers. The sweetness could almost be tasted. We could sense our Uncle's disappointment.

'"I wish he could win first prize," I said to Nati.

'Nati was deep in thought. "This time he will," she said.

"'How can he?' I asked.

"'We're going to help. We'll pinch Maximo. Without Maximo, he'll never win,' she said. I did not like the idea. It would be cheating. She said never to mind that; Old Martin should not be so greedy. He should let Uncle win sometime. Nati was determined. That seemed to set the balance right, and I was persuaded.

'Old Martin went home every evening when the village clock struck six. We lay in wait near his field and as soon as he had gone, we sneaked into it fast and out of it faster still, with Maximo in a Hessian sack. On the way home we encountered a group of gipsies by a narrow canal used for the irrigation. A tall, swarthy woman was holding a girl of about seven by the hair and shaking her violently.

"'I'll teach you a lesson for being careless. You dropped it. You get it back,' the woman said. The girl, who was the woman's daughter, must have accidentally dropped a frying pan into the canal. She was crying, refusing to jump in. But the mother said, "You'll get that frying pan even if I have to drown you." The woman was in a fury and, dragging her daughter by the hair, threw her into the water. The canal was deep enough to come up to the girl's forehead, and she was too frightened to get under the water. In spite of that, she tried several times without success and every time she came up without the frying pan the mother pushed her head back into the water. We watched with horror. "We'd better run," I said, anticipating being at the receiving end of the woman's wrath.

'But Nati was not anticipating this. Running and jumping into the canal, she retrieved the frying pan and handed it to the woman. "Out of here, you little bastard," she said, snatching the frying pan from Nati's hand and chucking it into the water again. "She dropped it she'll have to get it back. Away with you. You interfering little bastard. Away with you or I'll get El Moro to cut you," she shouted at the top of her voice. There was nothing else to do but run.

'Maximo was in our hands. "'Now we've got it, what are we going to do with it?"

"'We'll eat it. That's what we'll do." Nati as determined.

'And so we did! Uncle Patricio was as happy as a sandpiper, having achieved the dream of his life. Old Martin was hopping mad at the disappearance of his prized specimen. Suspicion was in the air. One day it burst like a fun fair balloon when we inadvertently stumbled into Old Martin on a path near his field. Nati nudged me and started to run.

'"Not quite so fast, you little thieves. I know your game. What did you do with my Maximo?" Shivers went down my spine as we replied in unison, "Nothing… we did nothing, Uncle Martin." Calling him uncle seemed to soften him a little.

'"I know you stole Maximo. You were the only ones who knew where it was." Then he put on a sinister face. "Do you remember what I do to trespassers?" Our mouths were sealed. "Have you lost your tongues? I'll refresh your memory. I shoot them. I shoot them dead and they never come back." He took a few steps backwards. Then stopped and cocked his shotgun.'

'Were you scared?' Alfonso and I wanted to know.

'Very! He gave us another sinister look. More sinister than the previous one. This time a wry smile distorted his mouth, accompanied with the closure of his left eye, so tightly so that we thought he would never be able to open it again. "Yes. I think I'll shoot you. And cut your heads off after and hang them on the roof of my cabin for the vultures to pick at." I felt a fit of giggles coming. The whole thing was too comical to be true. Nati listened to him, hoping that he just wanted to scare us. A few moments after, aiming first at Nati, then at me: put the shotgun down and roared, "What did you do with it? The truth, and I'll let you go."

'Some almost inaudible words came from our lips. "Ate it… we ate it." That seemed to appease him, and we ran faster than ever before.'

'Did Uncle Patricio ever know this?' We wanted to know.

'We told him. He laughed. To be fair, I gave Old Martin the five duros and kept the medal of La Virgen de la Granja. We're really good friends. He's just a softy who likes to torment me.'

Guernica

April 1937. The town of Guernica, in the Basque provinces had been bombed and pretty well destroyed by German aeroplanes. My eldest sister, Adelaida, a schoolteacher, was there during the bombing. The air raid took people by surprise. Hundreds fled en masse to the surrounding open fields to escape the bombs, but even there, the attacking aeroplanes relentlessly pursued them. Many died. A friend of my sister's called Pilar Zulaica, another teacher, who was heavily pregnant, died in childbirth amidst exploding bombs.

Adelaida and hundreds of Basque children were taken as refugees to France, where my sister spent the three years the Civil War lasted. Most of the children where taken to Pau, a small village near the Pyrenees, where Adelaida continued to teach. I still remember the letters her pupils, some of them of similar in age to mine, sent me written on yellow paper, some in ink, others in pencil. I was privileged to be their teacher's little brother.

When the war finished and Adelaida returned home, she avoided the topic of Guernica, so we learnt no details from her, an eyewitness who saw the tragedy unfold and suffered its effects to the full. Now with the wisdom of advanced age, I understand her silence. The memory of carnage, the reality of being attacked in such unprecedented manner, and above all, seeing her friend Pilar Zulaica and her baby dying at birth were tragedies better confined to the past.

I remember Adelaida as a tall, svelte woman who took good care of me till her departure for Guernica. A visit to the Alfredo Calderon, a Madrid school where she used to teach, has remained a vivid memory in my mind. I must have been five or six and had never seen the inside a school before. The Alfredo Calderon was a new building, with large windows and spacious classrooms. But an occasion which should have been a joyful one ended in tears. I was overwhelmed, I should imagine, by being surrounded by many of my sister's colleagues wanting to welcome Adelaida's little brother. I cried and cried and stamped my feet, and nothing would calm me down. Not even a carpentry set that Don Gali gave me in an attempt to restore my confidence. A colouring book followed, which aggravated my condition even further.

Years later, Adelaida related the episode to me and confided that Don Gali and herself were very much in love and planning to marry. But that was not to be. The war separated them, and Don Gali died in the front line.

It was not only the Basque children who were sent abroad as refugees. A similar fate almost befell on Maria and me. My sister Martina thought it would be safer for us to be sent out of the country, perhaps to France. My mother, wisely, opposed this. Martina must have made contact with somebody at a nearby *guarderia*, a place similar to a home for children that dealt with these matters. One afternoon, a well-dressed man came to see us. We did not like him from the start. He smelt of cologne and had a pencil-line mustachio across his upper lip. And when he spoke, he let his words leave his mouth in a gloopy way.

During his visit we sat as usual around the dining room table. Maria and I next to my mother. Martina next to the smarmy man.

'Your children are all skin and bone.' He was right. 'There's little food here.' Right again. 'We can take them abroad to a better life, and when the war is over they'll return.' He gave us one ounce of chocolate each to show the kindness of his heart. He had sweaty hands.

The more he exulted the benefits of taking us away, the stronger my mother mounted her opposition. Maria and I, with a child's natural intuition, knew that that was not for us, and had we not been brought up so stoically, we would have been upset.

We knew there was a war going on and that food was more than scarce, but we did not realise that we were just skin and bone. We perceived things in a completely different manner, one that enabled us to go to school, play, be with our friends, be cold and hungry, go to the shelter when the sirens sounded their warning, and survive without ever thinking about it.

Memories

The war imprinted me with a recurring nightmare that I have suffered since childhood, and it makes its horrendous appearance when least expected. Day or night. It shows no preference.

I am walking on the open road. It is early evening, already dark. A convoy of lorries carrying soldiers drive past, an endless serpent of detached links, brown and green, noisy with the hollering of the horde.

There is machine-gun fire in the distance, spraying bullets and terror, and nearby hand grenades explode and kill. And I walk on automatically, at the rat-tat-tatting sound of destruction. I see nothing but derelict buildings, piles of rubble, broken glass, twisted metal, and sometimes fire that burns with dirty flames, coughing up smoke that refuses to float in the air like the remains of an amorphous giant, ponderous in movement, helpless in its efforts.

The noise of bullets and shrapnel rams its threatening rods through my ears and wraps itself around trees bare with autumn, hanging from branches, waving a futile protest in the wind that nobody hears, a wasted message. When only the desolation of destruction is palpable, death is a welcome deliverance.

Bullets slice the air in a stormy rain of metal that seems endless, and I take cover behind a mound of debris and mud by the side of the road. What is now a mound of debris and piles of broken bricks was, not long ago, my old school. I crouch and slip on something warm and wet, and my hands feel the tackiness of half-clotted blood, the glutinous feel of human fluids. I look down. A pair of glassy eyes stare back at me. It is an unmistakable sign of death, the recent death of a man. My hands plunge into his belly, which has been slit open, exposing his intestines, making my hands bloody and pussy. The smell of death reaches my nostrils. A familiar smell now.

I look at him and watch a trickle of blood still flowing from his forehead where a piece of shrapnel has penetrated the front of his skull and wonder how much more blood will flow from there.

I look at this man without feeling. My heart is cold. There is no emotion. The war has taken all that away. One more corpse. One more! Does it really matter? But I wonder what happens after death. Was this man, like me, devoid of all feeling? I know he is now.

One more corpse! I am used to this. I am aware of this. But what I am not aware of – not yet anyhow – is that one day, when the carnage and destruction ends, these images will, like Lazarus, be resurrected to haunt me. Then all this to which I am immune now will become vivid images of terror that will remain with me throughout my life like the coagulating blood that covers my hands.

But now I am cold and hungry. Lost. Alone. The rain of bullets continues and I find myself standing up and walking amongst the whistling projectiles, defying their course.

'Careful. Be careful, there. Stop. Stop.' I hear a voice. A voice... a voice that echoes behind me.

I walk on in the dark. It is difficult to see in the poor light. Evening has turned into night, dark and dismal. I ignore the voice and walk on until something grabs my arm. A man comes into the dim penumbra of the street and the voice continues to say something I cannot quite understand.

'An uncovered manhole. We are working on it. Walk on the other side of the pavement.'

For an instant I am confused. The man looks puzzled. He is a utilities worker from the council trying to put things right. He will soon put the manhole cover in place and nobody will fall in and get injured.

It's bizarre how the past comes back into the present. It's bizarre how when I walk at night, just for the privilege of walking, memories of years past come to haunt me, to torture me with the vivid reality of what happened long ago. And I still remember. Day and night. More horrid at night.

Now when the sun shines life is more bearable. Sometimes! Even if the sun does not show its face, the light of day, however dim, wards off the ghosts, the funereal images, the sounds of torture, the macabre past that was, the stench of miasma that emanated from decomposing cadavers abandoned by the road side, in fields, in the most remote places, and in familiar ones.

Now that the voice of the man has brought me to reality, I feel a sense of relief. I know that the present has replaced the military lorries with buses, the horde of soldiers with lively passengers, the machine-gun rumble with that of heavy traffic. I know that at the end of the street where I am walking, I will be able to turn round and head for home. And once again, I will try to shake off the memory that accompanies me everywhere, chained to me like a convict. This will not abate the pain. The night will be long, I know. Only hope will abate the pain. The hope that at daybreak, the light filtering through my window will dampen the suffering till evening.

    Just till evening.

Pacho's Death

During a break in the lessons at the Larrumbe school, waiting for Doña Amalia to make her appearance, bringing with her her bouncy well-upholstered anatomy, El Militino, Juanito, Carlota, and I had a serious discussion regarding rocket practice. Juanito's eyes shone with anticipation.

'I tell you, without the hole on the top side our rocket will fly over the fence to the other side of the canal.'

This elicited smiles of approval from the rest of us. 'And I won't have to light any matches,' Carlota said, relieved.

So it was arranged that as soon as I could get hold of some calcium carbide we would go to the Canalillo with a few empty cans of pilchards and bomb the far side of the canal with our rockets.

Doña Amalia made her entry into our classroom with some delay. Her face bore the imprint of bad news. Something tragic must have happened; her hanky was busy travelling from her eyes to the pocket of her skirt.

The lesson continued for a while as it normally did, but there came a point when she succumbed to tears and remained in her chair, speechless. Finally, she made a grave announcement: 'Something very sad happened yesterday. Pacho got killed in the Canalillo's cave.'

Pacho was a boy who attended one of the classes for older pupils. We only knew him by sight, but hearing the sad news had an impact on the four of us.

Doña Amalia explained very little about the circumstances. It appeared that Pacho was playing with friends in the cave. The accident happened when the roof of the cave collapsed and killed Pacho. That was Doña Amalia's version.

Cousin Angel knew what really happened. Pacho was not on his own. Two friends were with him. Pacho and friends discovered a hand grenade and pulled the pin out causing it to explode. Their bodies had to be dug out by the fire brigade. All three died shortly after.

It was amazing how the death of one of our peers affected us. We were used to hearing about the killing of many soldiers, civilians, or members of the church, but Pacho's death was too close to home.

We did not go to the Canalillo for a while. The tragic event lodged itself in our minds, and in our imaginations, we reconstructed the collapse of the cave, how deep Pacho and his friends had been interred there.

'It could have been us,' El Militino said.

Juanito, his superior knowledge of weaponry on display, commented, 'It would not have happened to us.'

'A grenade can go off even if you look at it.' Carlota was also knowledgeable about such things.

'You have to pull the pin out to make it go off,' Juanito explained.

One day we decided to resume our aborted rocket operation. A lump of calcium carbide was in my pocket ready and waiting to be used. There were two empty cans of pilchards in El Militino's hand. Carlota was attired in the Raven's outfit, and Juanito had an aluminium water bottle hanging from his trouser belt. The four us, arms resting on each other's shoulders, marched to our destination. This time we went silently in order not to arouse suspicion.

The cave had been completely razed to the ground – a wise measure to avoid a repeat accident. The sand and rubble with which it had been built had been loaded in sacks and carted away to be used as protection from snipers and enemy bullets.

The Canalillo did not look the same having lost its main attraction. We stayed away from where it had stood and found a convenient mound to install the rockets. Two holes were made and small lumps of the carbide dropped into them.

'We'll shoot one at a time.' El Militino had a good sense of order.

Water was added to one of the holes and immediately covered with the pilchards can. A few moments later a subdued hissing, a bang, and the can took to the air. Over the barbed-wire fence it flew, to land on the other side of the canal.

We cheered as a well-trained chorus, and the second rocket was fired with the same success. Juanito won our admiration once more, now that his new invention had met with success.

We still had some of the carbide left but no empty cans. 'We'll need to go to the other side and retrieve the cans,' I muttered. My enthusiasm was too strong to think of danger.

'We'll draw lots,' Carlota said, in support of my idea.

'Juanito will devise a way to get across.' El Militino knew how to choose his man.

Juanito gave Carlota a persuasive look. 'You can swim, can't you?'

Carlota had boasted many times of how much she enjoyed swimming in La Poveda, a small stretch of river near Madrid. I, too, remember going there with my father and the rest of the family before the war. She had made so much of her swimming that I somehow had surmised it was all in her imagination.

'The water is cold.'

'But it's summer.'

'My mum will skin me alive if I wet my dress. It's better if Manolo does it.'

So I was forced to volunteer. The canal was narrow, perhaps some five feet across. We did not know the depth. We made a chain with our belts for safety and after widening a gap in the barbed wire, three of us went in, leaving Carlota as a lookout. I was not a swimmer, but luckily, I could handle the water by dog paddling. We secured the end of the belt chain to my waist and I got into the canal attired in only my underpants to find that the water came hardly to my knees. A quick retrieval of the cans and an even quicker return to safety followed.

'We shan't do any more shooting across the canal,' Juanito ordered.

'We don't want to lose the rockets again.' Carlota was relieved at this narrow escape.

In the process of finding a more convenient place for our shooting, we discovered something that needed our undivided attention. 'Bullets! Those are bullets. And they are much larger that the ones in my mum's silver shooter.' Carlota was excited.

Lying on the ground, there were some half a dozen bullets. Judging by the size, they were rifle bullets.

'We'll take them with us and detonate them the next time we come.'

Juanito was not only an inventor, he also knew words like detonate. That put him in a category of his own.

'How are we going to dent-toner them?' we all asked.

'We'll stick a nail against the detonator and hold it with a bit of wire then we'll bash it with a stone.'

A brilliant idea. Or perhaps not so brilliant. Carlota and I exchanged looks. The day when her silver shooter went off and the bullet left a telltale hole in the roof of Ali Baba's Cave was on both our minds. In spite of that, we remained silent, sure that in the open ground there was no roof to make a hole in. The idea that the bullet could go through one of us did not count.

Malaga Wine and Mojicones

My middle brothers, Rafael, about sixteen, and Pepe, eighteen, were the black sheep of the family. They were unruly and dangerous. In families, especially large ones like mine, there is invariably somebody who strikes the discordant note. There are also factions of those who consider themselves friends and those who operate as a caucus. I was lucky to be the protégé of all my brothers and sisters, and because of this, I have often compared myself to Switzerland – always neutral in case of war.

Pepe, as he grew up, adopted a menacing attitude that often exploded into violence. On one occasion, he was about to throw Martina through the balcony because she had taken him to task for some wrongdoing. He would have done just that had my brother Salvador not come in at the very minute that he was dragging her by her arms within inches of the balcony bars.

On another occasion, he smashed a bottle of ink against the wall and threatened to pull the water supply pipe from the wall. These episodes were kept from my father for fear that Pepe might turn against him. My sisters cleaned up the mess on the inked wall so my father did not see it.

In those days, the water supply pipe was not sunk into the wall but fixed to it with flimsy tin brackets. Pipes were made of lead and exposed, as were the electricity cables and switches.

Pepe must have been called up and soon put in uniform, the typical khaki outfit, crowned by a silly little hat with a ridiculous tassel at the front. Why Spanish soldiers could not be given proper headgear like the Hussars or the helmeted Germans is something that has taken me years to understand.

The whole family was pleased with my brother's new soldier status, certain that he would be posted well away from the rest of us. That was not to be, and instead he was billeted in the barracks next the *Economato* (army food stores) where Carmina and I had requisitioned a small supply of lentils and bread – which almost cost us our lives and cost Uncle Fabian an injured back.

But there was some advantage having a brother in those barracks.

'Any day now I'll be put on sentry duty in the Economato gate,' he told Rafael, who rubbed his hands with anticipation. A strategy was devised, and between the two of them, a stream of supplies followed from the Economato to 41 General Oraa.

That day came and as planned, Rafael walked into the stores unseen in the late hours of the evening. Not surprising, with no artificial light that could be detected by the enemy or a friendly sentry.

The Economato was truly a horn of plenty. It could keep the family in food for as long as the war lasted and Pepe was manning the gate. But once in the stores, the prosaic idea of essentials such as lentils and rice gave way to frivolity when he was faced with shelves on which bottles of Malaga wine dressed in colourful labels seemed to implore him for their freedom. So a couple were freed. A bag of *mojicones* (buns) was added to the loot and brought home unnoticed.

The following day at midmorning Rafael and Pepe, in conspiratorial concord, led me into their bedroom, their index fingers on their lips, to command silence. There, on a bedside table, was an open bottle of ruby red wine, exuding a sweet aroma, in the company of a few mojicones and three empty bowls that were used for hot chocolate whenever Carlota managed to transfer supplies from her special sack into my pockets.

'Mojicones!' I exclaimed.

Malaga wine was poured into the bowls and the mojicones dunked into it. The three of us ate and drank with increasing gusto. My brothers talked as they feasted. I savoured the mojicones; with incredible capacity, they absorbed the ruby liquid that ran down either side of my mouth with every bite. A lovely warm feeling made me feel more and more comfortable. My brothers' conversation went on and on, becoming less and less understandable. After we finished the wine and mojicones, the room took to revolving like a kind of merry-go-round. I closed my eyes, hoping to stop the room from turning.

I think my sister Martina discovered my predicament and put me to bed, where I stayed till late afternoon. In my alcoholic slumber, echoes of her voice hit my ears. 'What have you done to Manolo?'

I woke up with a terrible headache, made worse by my father reading my irresponsible brothers the riot act. Although that episode did not go down at all well with my father, who was a stickler for discipline, he decided to accept it as a one-off.

There were, however, other episodes to follow. As the war wore on, my brothers absorbed the turmoil that surrounded us all. Violence was in the air.

Rafael was the first one to be in real trouble. A dispute with an older man ended with my brother being knifed in the leg. It happened in the very corner of the street, and nobody seemed to notice. My brother came home bleeding profusely. My mother was in shock. My father was fetched from the garage by one of my sisters. On the way back home, they called on our doctor, Don Juan Bonachera, who knew the family from old. I was not allowed into Rafael's room, where he was lying in his bed and muttering about revenge. I assumed that injuries by knife were reportable to the police, but judging by snippets of conversation I heard between my parents I surmised that my father had secured the doctors silence.

Maria had invented a short rhyme that described the doctor to a tee:

El doctor Bonachera
que hace la factura
por la escalera'

(Doctor Bonachera writes up the bill on the stairs)

Rafael must have been in a pretty poor condition, because Michito sat outside his bedroom for days. My mother spoke of fever and infection, and my father was beside himself with concern. Eventually, Michito entered the room and, as it was his custom, sat at the foot of the bed and announced the all clear, in his feline way.

I never knew what the dispute was about. On reflection I would put it down to my brother's short fuse. He must have told Pepe the whole story. Probably with some enhancement.

Pepe, who had an even shorter fuse, vowed to avenge his brother and set about to find the attacker around the neighbourhood. The older man was found, and a punch-up took place right outside the bread shop in the morning of a sunny day. There was great commotion in the street. Shouts and insults were exchanged, and so were punches and kicks. My mother was cooking. Rafael, Maria, and I ran to the balcony. We saw it all. Rafael muttered under his breath, 'That's the bastard.'

The surprising thing is that none of us were worried. Punches rained in every direction until a machine-gun sergeant intervened and the fight was aborted. This earned my brother confinement to barracks for an indefinite period of time and dashed our hopes of having supplies of much-needed food. I remember my brother Pepe as very strong who later in life became a wrestler.

These events had a severe impact on my father's quest for discipline, but there was more to come.

The Art of Queing

People were highly disciplined when queuing for food. The queues were always long and ever gaining length as the scarcity became more acute. A self-appointed minder took charge and, in turn, chose one helper for every ten people. This was necessary to keep prospective queue jumpers in check, as doing this was a mortal sin, even at a time when Catholics was considered the scourge of the people. Children and the old were normally excluded as not capable to handle the task.

Our flat was situated above the shops, providing an excellent vantage point to observe the goings-on in the street. It was sometimes a source of trouble when Sharazade, the Sultan, and their descendants bombed the pavement, occasionally hitting the odd passer-by, activating a chain reaction of blasphemy and damnation, or when one of us was too generous watering the roses that my mother grew in earthenware pots.

One day, chickpeas were in the offing in the shop below, and I was sent to collect our quota. There was a reason I was chosen for this most important job.

'Basilio likes you. He'll give you extra if he can,' Maria said. Basilio, the grocer, had a son my age. This was a guarantee for success.

'Make sure you remind him that there are twelve in the family,' my mother instructed.

I joined the queue as it was being formed. The minder, a curly-haired, tall man was in the process of appointing his helpers. As luck would have it, I should have been chosen as helper, but since children were not eligible for this task, I was pushed aside. A great big fat woman who smelt of onions took my place. There was something peculiar about this woman; she kept muttering words that sounded like 'fascists' and pointing to our balconies, and every so often she pushed me out of the queue with her great big bottom. I wished my friends had been there with me, especially El Militino as the time was ideal for his gut's daily ritual.

My turn eventually came. Basilio, hair slicked back and shiny with brilliantine was wearing his standard manila-couloured overalls. He was ready to dispense chickpeas with his metal scoop, which was easily comparable to an extension of his hand.

'Manolo,' he said, greeting me with a smile. Maria was right. He liked me.

'My mother says to say that there are twelve in the family.' I was an obedient messenger.

'And you're the youngest one, aren't you? As if I didn't know it.'

The chick peas were kept in a deep square drawer behind him. The metal scoop was dipped into the drawer many times and made a clinking noise that I liked. It returned full of the yellowish stuff, hard as marbles, and was packed in a *cucurucho* (an improvised paper wrapper) made with an old newspaper. He gave me a wink of his eye and one extra measure.

'Gracias, Señor Basilio.' I addressed him as Señor Basilio, which was appropriate for a shopkeeper, and not as Don Basilio, which was a courtesy title reserved for career or upper-class people. Class distinction would prevail for better or worse.

I met the Great Big Fat Woman again a few days later, as a result of an unfortunate incident arising from one of my sisters overwatering my mother's flowerpots. Water always finds its way to lower levels and as true as day follows night, it progressed down to the first floor and onto the heads of several people waiting to go into the grocer's shop.

Interfering with a queue was tempting Providence, even in those Red days, when Providence was a forbidden word. A queue interfered with could become a rabid monster. I was unaware of this when I heard a loud commotion of people climbing the stairs and furiously knocking on our door. Disobeying my father's instructions, I opened the door with El Michito, faithful as ever, by my side. I was confronted by a group of enraged women, captained by the Great Big Fat Woman, who this time was openly using the word 'fascists' profusely. I did not quite know what was happening. Rafael did.

He suddenly appeared and dispensed several slaps on both sides of my face, accompanied by the magic words, 'Idiota, don't you know you must not water the plants when there're people in the street?' I was puzzled, but he reassured me later. Rafael had used the same technique that failed Poncio Pilato, but with much better results. Had the situation not been diffused by his clever intervention, things would have taken a very dangerous turn. Being called a fascist in those days could mean one could end up in a cheka or beyond.

I cried and hollered at the top of my voice, so much that some of the women asked for clemency. One of them even called me 'petal'. An endearing term much appreciated.

'The boy didn't know,' some voices said. 'He won't do it again,' said others. 'Don't hit him anymore; children will be children,' others added.

The deputation dispersed down the stairs. The Great Big Fat Woman was the last one to go. By then I had recovered my bearings enough to say, '*Tia gorda* (you fatty), your bottom is bigger than your head.' It was an illogical comparison, just a badly crafted insult. A raspberry accompanied my words.

'Disgusting little hooligan.' She disappeared from sight.

I do not remember if ration books were used for general foodstuffs such as pulses, rice, and vegetables but I do remember having a ration book for bread. It was the size of a notebook, with a number of squares to match the days of the month. The marking system underwent several changes. At first the baker pencilled his initial on the appropriate square when the bread was bought. This proved an invitation to cheating. Maria rubbed out the initial and we got a second bite of the cherry. When the baker was wise to this trick, his pencil marking was replaced by ink. There were no ballpoint pens then; fountain pens were used by the cultured. That excluded shopkeepers. So a nib holder and nib was put to the test. It was a failure. This spawned the use of a gimlet, with which a hole was made in the appropriate square. Much to our dismay, this was a perfect success.

When autumn came, bringing with it an abundance of *castañas locas* (horse chestnuts, or conkers), our balconies acquired a place in history by becoming a platform for battle against passers-by, especially those finding shelter from the rain under an umbrella. It never rained a lot in Madrid, but when it did, it seemed to activate a clarion call that Rafael and Pepe obeyed religiously. Out onto the balcony they went, well equipped with conkers. When an umbrella had the misfortune of being within range of my brothers' projectiles, the reddish conkers were unleashed onto the moving target. Because this took place in the dark of a rainy evening, the targets were not inclined to ascertain the nature of what had collided with the umbrella. Nobody had the curiosity to stop, put their umbrella aside, look above, and get wet.

In dry evenings, the target was more difficult to hit and so the aim had to be accurate, and a swift return to the room was a matter of urgency.

More events took place on our balconies. Uncle Jesus and his family lived in a flat across the street on the same level as ours. Cousin Jesusin and I often played with a small mirrors to reflect the sun on each other's faces. It was a great pastime in Madrid; the sun shone continually for some three months or longer, and the sky of a permanent blue made us wish for clouds and rain.

'We could send each other messages this way,' he told me.

'How?'

'We can learn the Morse code. I have a book.'

It sounded exciting. Juanito was not the only innovator amidst our friends. Cousin Jesusin also had great ideas. So we started practice and soon mastered the S.O.S. But we made no more progress. My brother Salvador happened to see us and immediately brought up the potential danger. 'You're not to play with mirrors anymore. If these idiots – the idiots being the Reds – see you, they may think you're sending messages to the enemy.'

Our game came to an abrupt end. I was used to things like this happening. Not long before, Don Cesar had been in terrible trouble when accused of using his pigeons to deliver messages to the enemy.

Our matchbox telephone, invented by Juanito, came to a similar abrupt end.

'You need two matchboxes and a length of string. First, you wax the string with a candle, then make a hole in each of the boxes, thread the string through them, and make a knot on the ends to hold the string in.'

'Is that all?' I was amazed.

'Then if the string is long enough, you can throw one box to Jesusin from your balcony and keep the other for you.'

'What happens then?'

'Jesusin will speak into his box, and you'll put yours to your ear and hear what he's telling you.'

A balcony-to-balcony telephone. A superb idea but a non-starter, because although General Oraa was not a wide street Jesusin's flat seemed a million miles away when we tried to connect it to ours with a piece of string. So I settled for a shorter distance, the length of our balconies. I gave one box to Maria, and we tried to speak to each other like that. We did have a conversation, but I fancy most of the sound was carried not by the waxed string but by the way we shouted at each other.

Again, my eldest brother Salvador warned us of the danger should the Reds decide we were in with the propaganda machinery of the enemy.

Later, I learned that it was not Juanito's invention and that the system can actually work if properly assembled.

The Radio

Of all the people I knew, only Carmina's family had a radio. I suspect Doctor Coronel also had one, but if he did, he kept it very much to himself. A cautious man, he did not want to give anybody the chance of accusing him of listening to enemy news. The wind of suspicion was ever present.

My father acquired a radio that had been left in a car as an unwanted object. It was promptly christened by Maria as the Groaner. The radio was mounted on a metal chassis and housed in an all-black case. Its front was covered in mesh of the same colour. Compared to the car radios of today, it was rather huge, measuring something like fifteen-by-twenty inches or larger. The electronic lamps were as big as electric bulbs. An accumulator, similar to a modern car battery, was necessary to supply the power. As technology advanced, the metal chassis was first superseded by printed circuits and the bulbs reduced to the size of acorns. That gave way to the incredible circuitry of today, which resembles a multitude of thin worms wriggling about to produce sound.

The accumulator had to be recharged once a week, so every Friday my father and Uncle Jesus would bring a newly charged accumulator from the garage. One of the mechanics made a bracket with a centre sleeve through which a metal bar was passed, and Father and Uncle, each holding one end, walked it home.

The Groaner took an inconspicuous place in the dining room and was only used at night. It was never used for music. My father and my brother Salvador listened to it every night at a low volume. It sounded like just a whisper from my bed. My uncles joined in on some occasions. Maria said they listened to foreign radios.

This huge radio remained in our flat for many years, but after the war ended, it was never used as a large accumulator was needed to power it. With my father dead recharging the accumulator became a no no. I tried to convert the Groaner to the mains without success.

Because of lack of money, we did not have a radio for quite some time. I must have been about fifteen when a friend of the family, who was a radio technician, scored where I failed. A new small case was found, and I believe, the old Groaner still works, almost seventy years after the war finished.

Salvador had not been looking his best for a long time. I remember the colour had gone out of his face. He had an intermittent cough that repeated itself when least expected. I saw him spitting into his handkerchief. The spittle tinted the handkerchief red, like when Maria or I got a nosebleed on very hot summer days. That was normal because of the intense heat. But Salvador's cough and the blood from his mouth was different. It spelt a kind of deep worry. We did not know about tuberculosis or consumption.

My sister Amelia, who entered the family after Martina, adored Salvador and was always ready to help him. He was particularly kind to her because of her disability, and she appreciated it. Amelia had the misfortune of contracting meningitis when she was a child, and although the illness was not full-blown, it left her hard of hearing and with abnormal personality disorders, which translated into constant moaning, complaining, and mistrust and made life hell. She hated Pepe as much as she loved Salvador, but she treated me with affection. I accepted her and all the difficulties she created, and to this day she occupies a very special niche in my heart.

I think she must have been the first one to spot blood in Salvador's handkerchiefs, and although this had been happening for a while it worried her. Salvador dismissed it as nothing serious until one day he suffered a copious haemorrhage. The word 'haemoptysis' became part of the daily vocabulary, as did 'tuberculosis'.

Passing by his slightly open bedroom door, I caught a glimpse of my brother sitting up in bed and coughing blood into a bowl that was soon completely filled. Amelia was by his side all the time. A doctor came, perhaps not Don Juan Bonachera, who saw my brother's chances as black. Coagulants were administered to stem the flow of blood, which took a long time to subside. More new words that I could not fathom out were exchanged between the doctor and my parents. 'Pneumothorax', abbreviated as 'pneumo', joined 'haemoptysis'. There was talk of hospital, received by the doctor with a vehement shake of his head.

'Impossible now, unless you know somebody,' I heard him say. 'Best we can do is rest and the coagulants. Raw liver if you can get it.'

Knowing somebody, somebody influential was the curse of the Spanish people then, through the years, and still is now. Unfortunately, Spain has always been the country of the recommendation. Without this, little can be achieved on one's own merit. I did not know this then. Life proved it to me, and it is a system that I abhor.

Even if we had 'known somebody', there were not many hospitals, and the general consensus was that people went to hospital to die, not to get better. Perhaps that was because you were not hospitalised unless you were at death's door.

Salvador's plight was discussed with Doctor Coronel, who dismissed the idea of pneumo as crazy and completely counter-indicated. These different opinions threw the family into turmoil. Finally it was agreed to keep my brother under absolute rest.

Doctor Coronel was not only a neighbour but a good friend. 'Don't tell anybody about your son's episode,' he told my parents. 'Tuberculosis is, to many people, like the plague. Also, without certain tests we can't arrive at the right diagnosis. The blood could have been caused by a form of fibrosis affecting a pulmonary vein.' My sister Martina explained this to me years after the event.

The decision that Salvador should remain at home came with some relief. As far as I know, nobody in the family had ever been in hospital, with the exception of myself. I was born in the Calle de O'Donnell Maternity, but my mother had the rest of my brothers and sisters at home. Childbirth was a natural event then, when families actually existed. Mothers passed their knowledge to their daughters, and in larger families, which was then the norm, the older siblings were taught the duties and responsibilities towards the younger children. My grandmother Martina was usually midwife to my mother. During Rafael's birth, however, due to my grandmother's absence, Salvador was midwife. Another of my brothers, the youngest of a family of ten, died when he was a few weeks old.

I was never told why I was born in the maternity rather than at home. Now, with the wisdom of age, I suppose it was because my mother was over fifty and there was enough money in the kitty to afford maternity fees. She recounted with glee that after my birth – I assume I must have been taken away from her for tidying up – an ugly and miserable-looking baby was put in her arms.

'This is not my baby,' she screamed. Babies were exchanged and peace restored. I have often thought, though not too seriously, what my fate would have been had the exchange not taken place. In all probability, I would have grown up within a normal happy family, where the violent outbursts of my middle brothers and constant antics of Amelia did not exist. But, I am really my parents' son, and my physiognomic stamp strongly supports it.

    I never knew my grandparents on either side. So I never had a grandmother to cuddle me or a granddad to tell me stories of times past. With so many in the family and with so much dissent, there was hardly the opportunity for hugs and kisses.

The Doll's House

There had been a few quiet days, free of the noise of war. Sirens had not wailed. Aeroplanes had not been seen.

One afternoon put an end to that. We were playing ludo at Carmina's. There was no Carlota at this game, so Doña Carmen took her place, making a foursome with Maria, Carmina, and myself.

Suddenly there was a very loud bang. The block shook. The ludo board and counters fell off the table. Furniture moved about as the shaking continued. We heard the noise of cascading rubble, not unlike the unloading of building materials; stones, and bricks from a gigantic truck. The lamp in the center of the ceiling started to swing irregularly. The Pilot radio that had been playing on the background ceased to work.

We looked at each other, trying to conceal our panic. Carmina, ever protective, stood by my side and held me.

There had been no warning. No aeroplanes disturbing the sky and above all, no bombs exploding.

'Must be an earthquake.' That was Doña Carmen's explanation. Visibly perplexed, she did not know what action to take – stay put or leave the flat.

The block continued to shake. The noise became more identifiable – an avalanche of rubble cascading from up above, a continuous stream of it hitting the ground.

Doors to flats opened. Neighbors noisily made for the stairs, rushing down to the improvised shelter. Nobody knew what was happening. Many voiced their opinions.

'Must have been a bomb,' said one.

Somebody disagreed. 'No. Not a bomb. A buried mine!'

A white haired woman disregarded the danger of invoking the Virgin and started to pray. 'Oh, Virgen Maria, save us. Don't let the children die.' In the bloodthirsty environment that surrounded us, that was asking for real trouble, but in the circumstances, nobody took much notice of her. Only one man muttered, 'Amazing what fear can do for you.'

Doña Carmen decided to join the others, and all four of us started our journey down.

'Manolo, you stay with me. Don't be afraid.' Carmina held my hand rather tightly as we trotted down. When we reached the first floor we could see a cloud of thick dust through the landing windows. An acrid smell made us cough and our eyes were watering.

It was not easy to make the final progress on to the street, moving with the crowd of neighbors. Many were impatient, others just scared, trying to get out. When we reached the street, things were no better. The dust had become a curtain of fog that prevented us from seeing the opposite side. Our mouths became pasty with the taste of the polluted air. The contingent of neighbours was reinforced by others milling around.

Fire engines promptly arrived. The street was cordoned off. The noise and dust settled eventually. Members of our family formed a group of our own. My mother was obviously silently talking to Saint Anthony of Padua. Judging by her countenance, she was not very pleased with the Saint. I was sure she was recriminating him for allowing certain things to happen.

So what did happen that afternoon that interrupted our ludo game? The whole façade of the block facing Calle Castello collapsed and fell onto the street below, leaving that side of building open like a giant doll's house.

We went across the street to have a better view and stationed ourselves outside Señor Brigido's milk shop. The debris covered the whole street, including the pavement alongside the Asilo de las Mercedes, once a convent, now converted into a first-aid post with large red crosses painted on the roof.

The cordon extended from the corner of our streets, between General Oraa and Castello, till past Uncle Fabian's block. We curiously gazed at the bizarre image the building presented. Exposed furniture was strewn out of their proper places, pictures were askew, some hanging from a corner, others smashed against the floor. There were no kitchens or toilets on that side; they were relegated to interior rooms. On one of the floors, a bed balancing on the edge attracted people's curiosity.

'That's my bed up there,' a woman sobbed.

Miraculously, most of the contents were intact, with the exception of items housed by windows or attached to the now-missing wall.

Don Cesar and Marina were the last ones to leave the building and join us outside the milk shop.

'Have you got my tablets?'

'Yes, Don Cesar, they are safely in my pocket.' She called him Don Cesar in public to obscure the fact that they were living together unmarried, which was frowned upon even under the communist ideals of the Reds. The tablets, I assume, were painkillers.

Part of the terrace where the pigeons were housed was now free-standing, having lost the support of the main wall. That was the very place were the nests were placed. Don Cesar looked at it with horror. 'If that collapses, it will ruin the nests and the fledglings will fall to a sure death,' he muttered to himself.

The corner outside the milk shop gathered quite a crowd. Auntie Ignacia and Jesusin joined us. El Militino and his father also joined us. His vegetable shop was only a few paces away, so they had been at the scene from the start.

'Manolo can stay with us, Doña Maria Antonia,' El Militino Senior offered, anticipating re-entry difficulties.

Luckily our side of the block, which faced Calle General Oraa, was unaffected.

El Militino announced proudly, 'I was in the shop when it happened. Saw it all from the beginning. Where's Carlota?' We were worried about her. We searched the crowd, but there was no sign of our friend. Doña Carmen, who had watched our worried faces, made enquiries amongst our neighbors. Apparently she was visiting an aunt with her mother. Their flat faced Calle Castello and was one of the doll's house sites.

Behind our backs, we heard a voice say, 'Some of the neighbours will have to be re-housed.'

I watched my mother's face showing deep worry at the thought that Carlota could have come to harm. Now that they had become the best of friends and that Carlota no longer was a true descendant of the Devil, she was willing to let her share Maria's bed. But in our flat we were already crowded and there was no room for her mother. I could see she was tempted to speak earnestly to Saint Anthony when help was at hand.

Doña Carmen to the rescue. 'Carlota can stay with her mother in Ricardo's room, now that he's away with the troops.'

Juanito was amongst the missing. 'His dad won't let him come out,' El Militino said, knowing about our friend's family hierarchy.

The firemen, in their dark blue uniforms brightened up with gold buttons and shiny helmets, busied themselves with the debris. A Big Cheese arrived with two more men. Through the portal and up the stairs, they disappeared.

Time was marching on. There were only a couple more hours to nighttime and darkness. No artificial lights were allowed, in order to avoid being spotted by the enemy.

We would camp out with Auntie Ignacia if need be, packed like sardines. Everybody was in suspense. After an endless wait, the Big Cheese and his cohorts reappeared, brushing the dust off their uniforms. An announcement was made: It was safe to go back to the flats facing General Oraa. We did not have to camp out with Auntie Ignacia and the others.

Flats facing Castello would be fairly safe, provided the exposed rooms were condemned. To make certain this was adhered to, he said, 'My men will block the doors to those rooms.' His bombastic tone of command still rings in my ears. Carlota and her mother were pleased to accept shelter with Doña Carmen in Ricardo's room until the blocking of the doors was completed.

Clearing the debris was planned for the following day. Neighbors were encouraged to collect any wood found amongst the debris. My brother Rafael took good note of that and joined the firemen to clear the street. He collected a lot of wood, mainly beams, most of them decayed with time and the elements. According to Uncle Jesus, this was the cause of the catastrophe. He explained that the block must have been constructed with secondhand materials that in all probability, originated from demolished buildings. Rafael acquired a long-handled axe and chopped enough wood to feed the kitchen range for some time.

When we returned home, Michito cautiously emerged from under a bed as if he was wondering what on earth had happened.

Little by little, things settled. Carlota pushed a 'secret' note through the door, summoning me to Ali Baba's Cave. The gap through which we used to enter had narrowed, making access impossible. Don Cesar came to help and removed some of the *cañizo* (a mixture of canes and plaster) that had moved with the avalanche. Inside, the buckets and cushions on which we used to sit must have been rolling around, coming to rest by the wall. The bullet hole had closed. We looked at each other and laughed, happy that our hiding hole was intact.

'Perhaps I can borrow my mum's shooter again and make another hole,' said Carlota the mischief planner. Then, the homemaker took over, and after tiding up the place, we stepped onto the terrace. Don Cesar, with the help of the firemen, had moved the nests to a safe place away from the main wall.

It took a few days to clear the debris. When this was done, the pile of sandbags protecting the improvised shelter was made higher. An additional pile was added. The demolished façade was not rebuilt until well after the end of the war.

Nobody was killed or even hurt in the commotion. All in all, it was a miracle.

La Carcel Modelo

The spectre of war marches on, making its presence felt in the most unexpected situations. Some seventy years later, the conflict finished, but it was never truly put to rest. Margarita, a friend from Madrid I met many moons ago in England, told me an intimate story that rekindled painful memories. Her family, doctors and lawyers tainted with the unpardonable sin of sympathising with right-wing ideas, suffered the most inhumane persecution. To be accused of being right wing was enough for incarceration and often execution.

La Carcel Modelo (the model jail) is but a speck of dust in my memory. The grown-ups mentioned those three words in tones of despair. It took me a long time to learn that they stood for torture and assassination. The need to know more eventually compelled me to do a little research. Carcel Modelo was an appropriate name: when the building was erected in the nineteenth century, it was considered a model for penitentiary reform. This was not the case during the Civil War, however. Milicia men occupied the jail and on August 22, and 23, 1936, set about executing the prisoners – both political and military – including Republicans with right-wing tendencies, ex-Republican ministers, and generals. About thirty inmates were executed in those two days.

To disguise the assassinations by the militiamen, the government instituted even more bloodthirsty measures. A Committee of Control, formed mainly by members of the Frente Popular (popular front), a communist core, was created. La Guardia Interior (internal watch) was handed to the Milicias de Retaguardia (rear guard), which replaced the equivalent of prison officers. This gave free reign to the two new bodies to facilitate the infamous *sacas* (illegal removal of prisoners for execution), which took place during November 1936. The press was forbidden to mention the goings-on in the jail. Many of the prisoners perished in the carnage of Paracuellos del Jarama near Madrid, with thousands of other prisoners from other jails who were believed to have opposed the Republican government. Those were also members of the armed forces who refused to defend the Republic, falangists, members of the clergy, right-wing activists, and, in general, people suspected to have ideas conflicting with the status quo, the great majority of whom had been detained without formal accusation and not allowed legal help.

Margarita's story is a tragic one.

'My mother brought me into the world one November evening at the cost of her own life. According to my Aunt Teresa, something had begun to go wrong with childbirth late that afternoon. Under normal circumstances my aunt would have helped with the delivery like a midwife.'

This was a normal thing in those days, when mothers educated their daughters in this fact of life. My family is a good example. Granny Martina officiated as a midwife for my mother, and even my brother Salvador assisted on two occasions.

'My mother started to haemorrhage before delivery. Time was of the essence. An ambulance was needed. My aunt reached for the telephone, but the line was disconnected. The curfew was already in effect, so no one was allowed out of their flats. Auntie Teresa, ignoring the implications, which could be fatal, went out into the street in the hope of finding a way to take my mother to hospital.

'In the street a young soldier – one of many enforcing the curfew – ran to her, rifle at the ready. "My sister is about to give birth. She's haemorrhaging badly. We need an ambulance," she pleaded.

'The human instinct touched the soldier's heart.

'"Is she alone upstairs?"

'"All alone. We need to take her to hospital without delay. Otherwise she'll die."

'"Her husband…"

'"In jail."

'Suspicion crossed his face.

'"La Modelo," my aunt volunteered. "Without conviction," she added in a pained voice.

'"Wait here," the soldier answered and quickened his pace down the street, leaving my aunt in a state of anxiety, not knowing what would happen next. Her mind clogged up with fear. Moments later a police patrol car arrived, bringing the young soldier and two other men.

'"They'll take your sister to the Red Cross post." He pointed at the two men. "I wanted to accompany you but permission has been denied. I was a medical student before this mierda (shit) started. Good luck."

'Refreshing to know that sometimes in adverse circumstances there is somebody who lends a helpful hand as the young soldier did, knowing full well that his own skin was at risk.

'We hurried to our flat, stumbling up the unlit stairs. My mother, in agony and almost lifeless, was put on a chair and carried downstairs, leaving a trail of blood on the way down.

'I was born to a dying mother shortly after arriving at the Red Cross post.

'In La Carcel Modelo, my father and his brother, Uncle Nicolas, who had been imprisoned for some weeks, were unaware of the outside world and in fear of becoming victims of the ominous sacas. One morning a militia man turned jailer entered their cell and read my father's name off a piece of paper. "Follow me." His voice sounded hollow – spent through articulating the same phrase too many times.

'Then a tight embrace. A broken goodbye that could be the final one.

'My father followed as he had been ordered, certain that the man was leading him to an execution squad or, more likely, to be shot by a sniper hidden from view. To his surprise he was taken to the controller's office. The controller, who was sitting behind his desk, stood up and shook his hand.

'"Your wife has died in childbirth."

'I presume there must have been some compassion in his voice as even the most callous of beings possess some feeling in their hearts.

'"The funeral will be tomorrow. You'll be allowed to attend." A pause. "Under guard, of course."

'A prolonged silence followed.

'"She delivered a daughter." Then, he gestured to the militia man – an unspoken order to take him back.

'Days later my father and my uncles were called out by a similar piece of paper, never to return to their cell. We never knew if they faced the execution squad or if they were simply shot by a sniper.'

Most of Margarita's family were wiped out during the conflict. No reason was given: just the suspicion of an ideal that was not particularly strong. But not everybody suffered from gloom and doom in the Republican-occupied part of the country.

Francisca, a Spanish woman now in her eighties whom I was introduced to by Margarita, told me a different story.

'I lived in Madrid until I came to England many moons ago. My father and, I imagine, the rest of my family were very much in favour of the Republic. When other countries sent troops to fight for the Republicans, my father became a chauffeur to high-ranking Russian army staff, including a general. I remember the general as a stocky man with a round face who took a shine to my father. Honeyed almonds and chocolate covered peanuts seemed to be his staple diet and often mine. His knowledge of Spanish was not brilliant, but with a small vocabulary he managed to tell me stories of his homeland.

'Things were difficult in Madrid. Food was scarce; we were in constant fear of being bombed. Using the general's influence, my family and I were evacuated to Valencia.

'We fell in love with the town the moment we arrived. Food was plentiful. The streets were adorned with so many flowers that I thought I had died and was in paradise.'

Obviously Francisca had a better time than most under the Republicans. However, in war, especially in a civil war, nobody wins, and hard times for her father loomed on the horizon. When the conflict ended, he was put in jail for working for the Reds.

There is one thing the Spaniards will resent: foreign intervention in their country—a feeling that, in my view, is shared in almost every country.

Francisca's father, not a fighting man, paid for his interaction with foreigners by losing his freedom as a result of a conflict he, like many others, did not engineer.

Typhus and Smallpox

I was with Carlota in our hiding hole. She had brought the little basket which, on the memorable day of the shooting, had carried her mother's silvery pistol. For a moment I feared she might have borrowed the gun again to reinstate the hole in the roof. This time the basket looked rather full and I wondered what she had put in it.

'Doña Marina has given me a very nice book. It's for the two of us, really. All full of colour pages. What do you think it's called? She opened her eyes wide and shrugged a little. 'Guess!'

'Dunno.'

She took the book out and showed me. *Ali Baba and the Forty Thieves.*'

'Brilliant!'

We sat on our cushion-covered buckets and leaned over the pages, heads together, hair brushing each other's faces. We marvelled at the coloured plates. The cover depicted a bearded man in a turban and a woman next to him attired in loose, flowing clothes. A veil that covered her hair draped around her face. The scene kept our eyes glued on that image.

'We can disguise ourselves to look like them. I've got the stuff.' From the basket, she produced a tea cloth and a long black veil.

'I'll make a turban for you with the cloth. The veil is for me. My mum wore it in the Augustines.'

Her mother must have been one of many who suppressed their beliefs to stay alive. Very much so in Carlota's mother's case. For somebody with religious tendencies, being married to a policeman was simply unthinkable.

The cloth was wound round my head, to my friend's delight.

'Do I look like a real Persian?'

'Almost. You also need something else to look like one.'

Out of the basket an ounce of chocolate came.

'I'm going to paint a mustachio and a beard; then you'll look like a real Persian.'

She warmed up the chocolate by putting a corner of the ounce in her mouth, having bitten off a small piece for good measure. She then proceeded to smear my upper lip and chin until she was satisfied that her work was well done.

'Yippee!. Now you look like the man on the cover of the book.'

Without a mirror in the cave, I had to take her word for it. Her transformation was simpler and, I thought, better. The veil covered her from head to almost her sandals.

'Now we can sit and read,' said Carlota, in command as usual.

'There once lived in a town in Persia two brothers, one named Cassim, and the other Ali Baba. Cassim had married a rich wife, but Ali Baba was poor and made his living by cutting wood, which he brought upon three asses into the town to sell.

'One day when he was in the forest cutting wood, he saw a troop of horsemen coming toward him. Fearing they might—'

Suddenly, the pained voice of Don Cesar calling Marina startled us. The reading stopped. Her hurried foot steps followed. We went with Marina to the terrace. Don Cesar was lying on the floor clutching at his stomach.

'The pain is severe. I knew it would happened sooner or later,' he wheezed with a faltering voice. Marina knelt to his side, then turned to us, 'Quick! Call Doctor Coronel!'

We ran to his flat only a floor below, but there was no reply to the ring of the bell.

'We need an ambulance!' Marina was in a panic.

'My mum is home. I'll go get her.' Carlota understood the urgency. She also knew that facing her mother all wrapped in the borrowed veil meant asking for detention. A long one, at that. A split second and the veil came off, landing in my hands. Automatically I hid it in a seed drawer. Carlota must have convinced her mother that the situation was serious, because her mother ran as fast as she could to the Red Cross first aid post and hospital across from our block. Carlota returned with the news. Between the three of us we managed to sit Don Cesar up, his back resting on the wall. I could see him become pale – soon quite ashen. His voice was more difficult to hear. In spite of that, a faint smile appeared on his lips at seeing me in my guise.

'He's not very well. Not very well at all,' explained Marina. It seemed a strange way to say it. Would she have said the same thing to grown-ups? I had seen people who were 'not very well at all'. I was familiar with that. It hardened my feelings, converting me in a spectator of life, not a participant. When I saw Don Cesar in that condition, a thought passed through my mind. If my friend had been in that afternoon, she could have dropped down with the wall.

Time ticked by slowly. At long last I could hear foosteps on the stairs. Two Red Cross men followed Carlota's mother onto the terrace, carrying a stretcher, which was just a piece of canvas fastened to two round wooden posts. No ambulance when the sick or injured could be walked to hospital.

Lying on the stretcher, Don Cesar called my name. 'Manolo. Goodbye, Manolo.'

'My god!'

We returned to Ali Baba's cave. The veil went back in the basket and so went my turban. We had another look at the book, a brief one this time.

'I wonder what happens next.' She was curious.

So was I. 'We'll find out tomorrow.'

'I'd better take your beard and mustachio off. This disguise is only for us. Must not waste any of the lovely chocolate,' she said as she started to lick my face, her tongue slowly sailing around my chin.

'Almost all gone.' Now her tongue concentrated on my mustachio and lips, giving me a tingle. 'Tomorrow we'll do some more of this.' Mischief lit up her face and I thought I saw her blush a little as the feeling of her tongue caressing my face lingered.

'Yes. Tomorrow we will. We will find out what happened to Ali Baba when he saw the forty thieves.'

But Martina had other plans for tomorrow and announced that tomorrow was vaccination day. Our get-together had to be postponed. The authorities were very much on the ball concerning health. Vaccines against smallpox as well as jabs against typhus were compulsory. At one point the certificate of vaccination was part of a person's documentation, and the police could demand to see it at any time.

Vaccinations continued all my student life, but, Spain being what it is, we did not truly have to have the vaccine if we did not want to. Doctors issued the certificate whether the vaccine had been administered or not. This was common practice between students. The only requisite was to pay the fee for the certificate, which amounted to approximately twelve pesetas.

The authorities had every right to be strict. There had been some cases of typhus which if not properly controlled could have reached epidemic proportions. This was prevalent in overcrowded and unsanitary conditions during wars and famines. The disease could be transmitted by lice, contaminated water, or by a carrier. Because of the possibility of lice, in the Larrumbe school all the boys were encouraged to have their hair cut at *rapa terron*, an essentially shaved head.

Juanito, El Militino, and I chose this method of avoiding lice, and to show solidarity, all three of us went to Faustino, the barber, whose shop was in General Oraa only a few paces from the vegetable shop of El Militino senior. Our shaved heads earned the three of us generous marks by Doña Amalia.

'I hope I'm not going to catch the "trifus" because I can't shave my head,' Carlota said, sounding concerned.

We reassured her that girls did not need to have their hair cut to prevent typhus. Perhaps we thought they were immune to it.

The typhus jab was administered at the Red Cross post close to home. I arrived there with my mother and all available brothers and sisters. We queued up with our left-arm sleeves rolled up. Then came the standard 'It's not going to hurt.' Finally the sting. It did not hurt on execution. The pain came later, and so did the fever that lasted a few days.

No sooner had we recovered, we made another visit to the Red Cross post, this time for smallpox immunisation. The nurses changed the 'It's not going to hurt.' to 'Just a little scratch'. Then something not unlike a writing nib scored my arm twice to prepare the ground for some bright green stuff, which was smeared on the scratches. I did not care for that, especially when I heard that if it did not take there would have to be a second helping of the same. Fortunately, the vaccine met with success. I and the rest of the family developed awful sores where the scratches had taken place – a sign of success that stayed with us for the rest of our lives.

Hygiene was also of paramount importance. Anybody visiting a patient in hospital had to produce a Certificate of Cleanliness obtainable in a bath house.

Maria eventually heard that Don Cesar had suffered a burst appendix, was operated on, and was recovering. She also heard that

Doña Marina had been to the bath house for her shower and certificate so she could visit him. After a while Don Cesar came back.

'I have seven lives like the cat. Still six left,' Don Cesar said upon his return. (Spanish cats have only seven lives, not nine like their English counterparts.)

Doña Marina also made a kind of shawl out of bright-coloured cloth and proper headgear for me, saying, 'You can wear them for your reading.' And so we did when we went back to the intimacy of Ali Baba's cave.

The Bullet Hole

Carlota was waiting for me, sitting on the triangular rest on the landing. In her hand was a long cane. With her index finger across her lips, she commanded silence and beckoned for me to follow.

'We've got to fix something.'

When we got into Ali Baba's cave, she pointed at the ceiling where the bullet hole was before the main wall of the block collapsed. It had since been closed because of the commotion. Carlota was obviously determined to reopen it as a memento of the day when the silvery shooter went off.

'We'll see the sky through it again.'

'See the sky?'

'And the sun will shine through it.'

I had learned to accept her reasoning, especially when she was set on something. I did not mention any negative feelings about it, like that the size of the hole would be far too small to see the sky through or even to let the sun shine in. Her heart was set on reopening that bullet hole, and that was all that mattered since I would do anything to please her.

So I took the cane and, standing on my upside down bucket, worked on the ceiling until the hole was reopened. Some plaster and a lot more dust came down during the operation, and Carlota, whose sense for detail had always amazed me, gathered it up with a hand brush brought for that very purpose and deposited it carefully in a paper bag for disposal.

She smiled. 'See? It's much nicer now.'

I agreed. The porthole, as we called it, had been restored. To celebrate our achievement, it was time to continue reading *Ali Baba and the Forty Thieves*.

'When they were out of sight, Ali Baba came down, and, going up to the rock, said, "Open, Sesame." The door at once opened, and Ali Baba, entering, found himself in a large cave, lighted from a hole in the top, and full of all kinds of treasure—rich silks and carpets, gold and silver ware, and great bags of money. He loaded his three asses with as many of the bags of gold as they could carry; and, after closing the door by saying, "Shut, Sesame," made his way home.'

'See, Manolo, the thieves' cave was lit by a hole in the top, just like ours.' Her eyes shone for a moment. 'We ought to make the hole bigger.'

The noise of falling debris interrupted her words; then we heard the agitated voices of Don Cesar and Doña Marina coming from the terrace.

Curiosity took us to the terrace.

'Part of the cornice has dropped down into the street,' Don Cesar announced.

'This is terrible. I hope nobody has been hurt!' added Doña Marina.

'Don't come out here,' we were told. 'An end of the terrace is unguarded'.

We could see that the parapet beyond the pigeon nests was missing. In the street there was quite a commotion as people looked at the damage from the opposite side. More chunks of masonry and glass from the miradores continued to come down when everybody thought the cascading was over. We quickly returned to our respective homes and said nothing of what we had seen.

My mother, in a silent praying mood, admonished San Antonio de Padua many times, I am sure. In the meantime, Michito arched his back every time a chunk of masonry parted company from the rest of the structure. Occasionally a shower of broken window glass emitted a sharp sound as it was converted into shards.

Maria and I observed most of the spontaneous demolition from the kitchen balcony, a safe place at the far end of the façade facing General Oraa.

It took a while for the cascade of debris to stop, but even when it did we could see a big chunk of the cornice suspended by something that looked very much like a thick rope, dangling outside the first floor mirador, making it impossible for anybody to go in or out of the block. A sword of Damocles waiting for a victim.

We were expecting the fire brigade to come in their uniforms and shiny helmets, which would be a welcome sight. Time passed and there was no sign of the fire brigade. It was an opportunity for the men and bigger boys in the neighbourhood to show their mettle.

Emiliano, a newly communistic infected local, my brother Rafael, Nicolas of the grocery shop, a coalman from the coal store a few paces away from our building, and others tackled the clearing of the debris. El Militino's father's cart was commandeered for the operation, and after an hour or so the street was cleared, leaving the dangling chunk as an unfinished problem. After much considerations, the men arrived at a decision as to how to bring it down to the ground: open the mirador window and push it down. Emiliano and Rafael were chosen to approach the inhabitant of the flat, the Italian Signor Bataglio, who lead them to the mirador.

Emiliano studied the situation. Pushing the chunk down was not an option, but an action of Alexander the Great came to his memory – the rope attachment comparable to the Gordian knot. Saw in hand and encouraged by the memory of the great emperor, Emiliano set about the cutting the rope until the chunk parted company and plummeted to the ground, not without first hitting the lower part of the mirador window and throwing a shower of shards into the room, cutting Rafael's hand in the process and later providing Doctor Coronel with a stitching job.

Jail and Scabies

A small eruption of skin appeared on the little finger of my left hand. It grew bigger in a few days, so, concerned, I went to show my brother Rafael. To my surprise I found him in front of the mirror in my mother's bedroom. The large bevelled mirror was mounted on the door of an equally large wardrobe that was used mainly by my sisters to store their dresses.

Rafael was posing in front of it with a black pistol in his hand, making all manner of sinister and menacing gestures.

'This is not a toy, Manolo. It's a real gun to shoot whoever crosses me.'

His attitude was meant to be frightening. I thought it totally idiotic and said nothing.

'I want you to go down the street as far as Maria de Molina to see if you can spot any strangers. Here is ten cents. You're on a mission. If you do it well, there will be more money for you. Not a word to your friends!'

I realised he was dead serious. Even at nine years of age I knew he, like Pepe, was prone to strange behaviour.

I went down the street as he'd directed, but my first port of call was the stand of Señora Felipa, an old lady in black whose pitch was set on the opposite corner of the street. The stand was a rudimentary shallow box supported by a folding stand, where she displayed her wares: tiger nuts immersed in a bowl with water; palo luz; and liquorice sticks and other sweets, including the coveted caramelos de café con leche (coffee and milk fudge) wrapped in shiny paper with the name Logroño, where they originated from, written across it.

Knowing that life could end at any minute I was fully prepared for death and decided to spend my ten cents on tiger nuts that Señora Felipa dispensed in a cucurucho made with a sheet of news print. I would like to have shared the nuts with Carlota, but that might have blown my cover. Fortified by my purchase, I patrolled my route until all the tiger nuts were gone. Then, I returned home with a happy belly and a devilish idea.

'Saw nobody strange, but I heard something. Two men were talking about searching the flats.'

An anxious look crossed my brother's face. 'What did they look like?'

'Tall. With hats and beards,' was the best I could engineer.

Rafael buried the pistol in his pocket and bolted down the stairs as if chased by the devil. I must have said something important. Searches were the order of the day, which is why it had come to my mind so quickly. My invention promised to keep the flow of ten-cent pieces from my brother's hand into my pocket and finally in Señora Felipa's earnings.

This hadn't solved the problem of my finger, though, and now I could not show him. Martina was also out, but I tried her when she returned.

'That's a wart, Manolo. Señor Aragón, the pharmacist, will give us something to take it away.'

That something was nitric acid.

'Make a little brush with a match stick. Dip it in the acid and very carefully smear the top of the wart. The wart will turn yellow and will fall off in a few days. And no, it will not hurt,' he emphasized, turning to me.

The matches were made with waxy sticks no bigger than matches now. The head was removed as soon as it ignited, leaving that end with a few strands similar to a tiny brush. A simple application made the wart acquire a darker tone as the days went by.

Either by fluke or simply because searches were so common, my fib became reality, and one day not much later, two characters of the secret police erupted into our flat. Contrary to what the grown-ups and my mother expected, they did not search high and low. It was something specific they were after.

'We know one of your sons has a pistol,' one of the agents said in an unfriendly tone, his body language menacing.

My mother went pale. I inadvertently looked at Rafael. So did my mother. It was an unfortunate automatic reaction. We were all silent.

An agent grabbed Rafael by the top of his shirt and shouted, 'You're a likely bastard to be playing with firearms!' Rafael produced a cynical smile that incensed the agent, who slapped his face several times.

'Leave my son alone. Can't you see he's only a boy?' Then turning to my brother, she said in a no-nonsense voice, 'If you have a gun, give it to the agent.'

There was no reaction from Rafael other than a look of defiance.

'Where're your other sons?'

'Two in the army. One ill with consumption.'

'Then the cards are stacked up against you. You little bastard. We know the pistol is here.'

'No pistol here!' That earned Rafael more clouts.

'You've been shopped. You've been shopped by the bastard who sold you the gun. I'm sure you know why. Tell me why before I break your neck.'

Still a defiant Rafael.

'You didn't pay him, did you? He also gave us a few leads. As we speak, other addresses are being searched.'

Minutes later a motorcycle with a side car stopped outside our home. The agent in the side car alighted and climbed the stairs. There was a rap, rap, rap on our door.

'That puta (whore), Natalia, had it in her laundry basket.' He said as he entered the room.

I recognized the gun as it was shown to the others.

Natalia was, according to rumors, a woman of ill repute who lived in Principe de Vergara, a beautiful street with a tree-lined boulevard only a few minutes walk from our home.

Rafael was either jailed or put in a correctional – I was never able to find out which – for a few months. Had he been a little older, he might not have escaped so leniently.

My wart kept on blackening more and more, still firmly attached to my little finger. One morning when I was feeding our pigeons, the Sultan seemed to develop an interest in it and started to peck at it until it detached, and into his beak it went. Surprisingly, it left no mark on the skin.

Rafael returned home having acquired a brand new vocabulary of terms learned while behind bars. He was also full of scabies, which I contracted.

Scabies was another curse of poor hygiene and confinement. I first noticed a persistent itching around my waist, which was dotted with small watery blisters. The itching, more severe at night, spread to the whole body. A visit to Don Juan Bonachera's clinic became necessary, and my sister Martina took me there.

'This child has got himself a good dose of scabies. A tiny, naughty mite is the one that causes the trouble. It burrows under the skin to lay its eggs. Then comes the awful itching.'

I did not much care for his explanation. I just wanted to know if he was going to dole out spoonfuls of medicine to kill the naughty, tiny mite.

'I have the very thing to stop the trouble this tiny fellow is causing.'

We came out of the clinic with a pot of belladona. Unfortunately it wasn't something to eat; instead, the belladona was to be spread all over my starved anatomy by Martina's skillful hands. Belladona is black and pungent, so every night for a few nights I was transformed from a pale skeletal creature into a black one. The scabies responded quickly to the assault, which put paid to my itching nights.

Tio Morales

Señor Morales, better known as Tio Morales, or as my father used to call him, Morales, was a corpulent man, awkward of movement and unpleasant in manner. He and his wife, Señora Paca, were the caretakers of 41 General Oraa.

Accommodation was provided for them in a small flat on the ground floor of the block adjoining the hall with a half–panelled, half-glass entrance door, behind which a bamboo curtain hid them from view. This allowed them to see without being seen, unless people really made an effort. It took me a long time to fathom out how they knew when somebody came in until Juanito, in his wisdom, put me right.

Morales and Paca held the fort twenty-four hours a day. There was no such thing as working hours for a job like theirs. The postman left the letters for all the occupants with them, and when any of the neighbours blessed with correspondence entered or exited the block, the caretaker's door would open swiftly and any correspondence put in the hand of the individual. There was not a lot of correspondence and no junk mail existed, so that part of the job was a light one. The postman only delivered registered letters or telegrams directly to the occupants of the flats. There was usually a tip for him.

On one occasion when my sister Adelaida wrote to us from France, the postman delivered the letter to the flat. My mother, grateful for the gesture, offered him a glass of white wine. We were assembled round the lunch table about to appease our hunger with a dish of lentils cooked in water without even salt. To our surprise the postman took a small sip of the wine and, with some disgust, returned the glass to my mother.

'Warm white wine will do my gut no good.'

Tio Morales reserved for himself more rewarding duties. The wooden staircase – no lift in existence – had a dark reddish brown banister that he shone with pride. A lot of wax polish went into it, which we greatly appreciated, though not for the reasons Tio Morales did.

The stairs were in a poor state, rickety in parts and showing signs of wear in others. Some rungs curved inwardly with age and use, but the banister was beautiful. The temptation to ride this beauty all the way down to the hall was irresistible to my peers and myself. The bigger boys rode it like a horse with ever increasing acceleration as they approached the bottom. Carlota and I preferred to bend over the banister and have an easy ride on our stomach.

Tio Morales seemed to have a sixth sense for detecting the banister riders and would wait in the portal to give a good dressing down to the unlucky ones who were caught. Afterwards, we would walk away and, once out of earshot, have a good giggle. Laughing to his face would have resulted in being turned over to our parents, which was too high a price to pay.

Tio Morales showed a particularly virulent side of his character with the lower classes like *la trapera* (the rag woman), who used to knock on every flat door once a fortnight offering to exchange crockery for rags or old clothes. My mother usually obtained some small jug or pot in exchange for discarded clothes from the family. Tio Morales's virulence reached a peak with the dustmen who every morning came to collect the rubbish. Like la trapera, they collected the rubbish left outside the flats. Tio Morales was always at the ready to tear a strip off them if they dropped any litter in the process of their job or if they dared to put dirty hands on his beloved banister.

My father was at the sharp end of his tongue one evening when, having no coal, wood, or even paper to burn in the kitchen range, he resorted to burning the remains of an old dungaree soaked in paraffin. Although a wonderful combustible to cook our lentils, it generated a great deal of smoke and an unpleasant smell. Tio Morales, having a keen nose and an even keener eye, climbed the stairs blaspheming at the top of his voice and venting all manner of threats, to which my mother replied, thin poker in hand, with God's damnation on his soul. My father intervened, and –once the three of them had given vent to their anger and the smoke had dispersed – put the row to rest.

On reflection, Señor Morales, who could well have been an army man in his younger days, was a great asset. The stairs and common sections were spotlessly clean; children were under control; neighbors engaging in shouting matches were reduced to silence under the echoes of his stentorian voice. There was strictly no whistling on the stairs. This applied in particular to Rafael and his friends. Pavements around the block were brushed every day as an extra activity that he imposed on himself for the sake of tidiness. When somebody died, it was he who set up a table in the hall covered with a black velvet cloth surrounded by white flowers. A ribbon was placed around it with an inscription bearing the name of the deceased followed by, 'Your neighbors will not forget you.' The portal, like most portals, had double doors. When somebody died, one door remained shut until the coffin carrying the corpse, which had been kept with the family, exited the block.

Winter was settling in with cutting winds and temperatures hovering at zero centigrade. We had reached the end of the line as far as combustible materials – something which affected everybody. One morning El Militino and his father came to see my mother.

'Doña Maria Antonia, my son and I and a couple of friends will be going to collect wood from a block of flats that was hit by a bomb a few days ago. Perhaps Manolo can come with us.'

With Pepe confined to barracks, Jesus in the army, Salvador with consumption, and Rafael back in jail for some undisclosed reason, the offer was very welcome.

'I know it's pretty cold but the children will enjoy it. Must wrap up well, though.'

My mother wasted no time in speaking to Auntie Ignacia, who mobilised cousin Jesusin to join the party. The following day, our group of eight made our way down Castello equipped with El Militino's father's small vegetable cart. Soon after we started on our trek I heard running footsteps behind me. It was Carlota attired Eskimo style in boots at least two sizes larger than her feet, a red woollen hat with a white tassel, and a coat that made her look like an inflated Michelin. Her attire contrasted with mine – a handed down coat from Rafael that had seen better times and was too thin to shield me from the cold.

The group stopped with Carlota's arrival.

'I want to go with Manolo,' she said in clear terms.

'Are you sure you want to come? We're going to collect wood for the fire. It's going to be hard work'

No comment came from my friend, but her expression was determined.

El Militino's father, head of the expedition was clearly tempted to mention the cold, but he refrained, studying her attire in detail. Nobody spoke for a while. Perhaps El Militino's father thought Carlota too frail for the task at hand. Little did he know how resourceful she was.

Carlota finally broke the silence. 'I'm coming with Manolo and El Militino.' That was final.

The three of us walked at the rear. Carlota, ever dutiful, produced three ounces of chocolate from her furry coat – one for each of us.

'Stay with us, Jesusin,' Carlota called and handed him the ounce of chocolate that she had reserved for herself. 'We'll share yours, Manolo.' And so we did, taking little bites at the corners. The chocolate tasted much better eaten that way. The cold increased with every step we took, and the sky became grey.

'I think we're going to have snow,' one of the men said. The comment seemed to encourage the first snowdrops to fall. It rarely snowed in Madrid, but when it did it soon turned into ice, leaving the streets covered with a slippery coat.

I observed that Jesusin, always full of tricks and fun, was now strangely quiet and visibly shivering.

When we arrived at the bombed site, El Militino's father took command of the group and allocated jobs. El Militino, Jesusin, Carlota, and I were told to collect the small pieces of wood and fill a Hessian sack with them. The grown-ups set about loading the cart with larger pieces, mainly broken sections of beams. The ones too long for the cart were cut into smaller pieces with a handsaw. The snowfall gained momentum, covering the debris and us. This did not deter us from our task. It became part of our enjoyment. Our faces were soon red with cold and activity, and our happy laughter rang out. Strangely, Jesusin was silent, his face purple and his hands shaking.

El Militino's father caught a glimpse of him.

'The cart is almost full. We'll soon finish here and go home,' he said with a softened voice.

Soon after, a loud explosion was heard in the distance and Jesusin fell to the ground, his whole body shaking. He was breathing alarmingly fast, and we could almost hear his heart thumping. El Militino's father bent over him. 'He's having a fit,' he muttered to himself. 'Come son, let's go home.' He turned to the rest of us. 'We'd better go.' Then he picked Jesusin up and carried him home.

'Is he going to die?' asked a worried Carlota. Neither El Militino nor I had the answer. We missed Juanito. He surely would have told us what we did not know.

We accompanied El Militino's father to Auntie Ignacia's flat. Jesusin's eyes were now closed, his breathing a normal whisper. Auntie Ignacia put him to bed with a wine bottle filled with hot water at his side to keep him warm.

'He's been having fits for a while now. Doctor says they could be triggered by fear. This never happened before this insane war.'

Arsenic

There was great concern about Jesusin's fits, which had increased in frequency and length. Auntie Ignacia had an intense council of war with my mother and decided that a visit to Doctor Don Juan Bonachera was needed.

'This boy is all skin and bone. He needs food more than anything else.' Doctor Bonachera paused as somebody does who suddenly woke up to reality. Food! A rare commodity. 'And a tonic. I'll give him a strong tonic.' A prescription was scribbled and taken to Señor Aragon, the chemist.

'This is powerful stuff, Doña Ignacia. One drop in water the first day, two the second and so on up to fifteen. Then, reduce the drops by one a day. Fourteen, thirteen, and so on to just one. This will put the colour in your boy's cheeks.'

A dark brown glass bottle contained the powerful stuff – a reddish liquid smelling of lavender and labelled Fowler's Solution. It was a concoction of arsenic and some other substances.

Carmina and I went to see Jesusin a few days after his fit. He was in cheerful mood, and he spared not one single detail of his visits to Doctor Bonachera and Señor Aragon.

'I'm on four drops. Look at my biceps.' He flexed his right arm to show us. We couldn't see any improvement but we lied. The important thing was that he was his normal happy self.

'Tell us a story,' Carmina requested, always preferring him to be serious rather than playing the clown.

'I'll do better than that. I'll tell you about when I went to Sequeros.'

As usual we sat on the edge of his bed in the cocoon atmosphere of his room while he stood in front of us, occasionally pacing with studied short steps, now and then resting his body in a wicker chair normally holding a sketch pad.

'Sequeros is a village near Salamanca where my father and my father's family originated.' Jesusin took a short breath. 'I went to

Sequeros well before this mierda started. No bullets flying around, bombs, hand grenades, or anybody wanting to kill you.'

Incredible that there could have been a time without any of that. For the past three years that had been the norm and for me, who had lived in that environment since the age of seven and had been immersed in that kind of thing because of circumstances, any other life was the stuff of fantasy.

'My mother sewed some money in the waist band of my pants for safe keeping since I was going to travel on my own. My father took me to the Estacion del Norte and boarded the train, where he selected two fat women who were traveling to Salamanca to look after me. The fatties smiled reassuringly as he left the train. My charges insisted I sit between them, and as soon as the train began to move, out of a basket that they guarded like gold dust came a potato omelet followed by peaches and a cylinder of *brazo de gitano* (Spanish version of chocolate roly poly).

Carmina licked her lips, longing for some of the feast now impossible to obtain.

'Was the omelet nice?' she asked.

'And all the other things?'

'Very. We munched all the way to Sequeros, where we parted with hugs and kisses.

'I stayed with Uncle Timoteo, who sported a large handlebar moustache like my dad. Uncle Timoteo runs the village school. Quite a big cheese, according to the locals. Being his nephew had its advantages – but not always.'

'Not always?'

'People stared at me wherever I went. It was a bit off-putting at first, but I soon got used to it. People were different there and so were most other things.'

'Like what?'

'There was only one proper street, which was also the main road. There was no water in the houses. It had to be fetched from the village square, where there was a huge fountain with four jets. The women brought the water home in funny-looking earthenware pitchers.'

'Is it true that they carried the pitchers on their head?' Carmina wanted to know.

Jesusin assented.

'Cats, dogs, chickens, even ducks, roamed around not taking much notice of anybody.' After a pause Jesusin added, 'No loo in Uncle Timoteo's house.'

'So, where did you go?' I was sure this was one his lies. How wrong I was.

'Every house has a corral with chickens. That's where you go. Mear (peeing) is easy. Poo can be a little difficult.'

Carmina and I exchanged glances. What was he going to tell us next?

'The chickens gather around you the minute you're on you hunches, waiting to peck the poo. Often they do that as it's coming out.'

A brief pause. Brief enough to discourage any questions.

'I soon got myself some friends. Isabel, Silver Bell; Gervasio, the Grasshopper; and Anton, Tomato Face. Life in the village was full of surprises. The first morning a cockerel woke me up singing at the top of its voice. A bit later I heard somebody blowing a whistle, and a herd of pigs appeared on the patch of ground close to the houses. All the pigs followed the whistle. When I saw my friends, I told them.

'"It's the Pig Man," explained Tomato Face.

'"Takes the pigs to the woods for acorns," added the Grasshopper.

'Silver Bell remained silent, looking at me, not the way the people of the village did. She couldn't believe that I did not know about the Pig Man.

'A journey to the woods sounded fascinating, and wished I could go with the Pig Man.

'"That's asking for trouble." Tomato Face offered that sensible thought.

'"The Pig Man never takes anybody with him,' contributed the Grasshopper.

'"Never talks either," ventured Silver Bell.

'"I'm going to ask him."

'"He'll never take you, anyhow."

'"You'll need boots."

'"And a hat."

'"There're snakes where he goes."

'"Vipers."

'"And scorpions. 'People die of scorpion stings."

'"Their belly goes swollen."

'"And the face, yellow."

'My friends were well informed.

'Silver Bell was frightened at the thought of my journey to the woods with the Pig Man and being stung by a scorpion or bitten by a viper.

'"He's weird," she said to reinforce her friends' points. And then, she added, almost like a plea, "Don't go, Jesusin."

'"I'd like to go, anyway."

'"And end up with a swollen belly and a yellow face?" Tomato Face sounded agitated.

'"He always looks miserable." Silver Bell disapproved of her friend's harsh statement.

'Nothing my friends said made me change my mind, and if the Pig Man did not want to take me, I would follow him. The following morning I waited for the whistle to sound, and when the Pig Man appeared, accompanied by the pigs, I approached him.

'"No. You can't come."

'But I was not going to take no for an answer. My mind was made up. I stood in front of him. He did not say anything for a while.

'Finally he said, "Need boots. Need hat." After that he went on his way, followed by the pigs.

'I could make a hat with a knotted handkerchief. Boots were quite another matter. I started to get worried. No boots. All those vipers and scorpions. My friends might be right. Especially Silver Bell. I could tell she was frightened. In a way I wanted to show her that I was not scared. I somehow imagined she would like that in spite of her fears.'

Carmina, full of feminine intuition, giggled in my ear. 'I think he liked Silver Bell.'

'Later that day we went for a swim in the river. Silver Bell got in the water in her flimsy summer dress; the rest of us were naked.'

'"Girls are funny," said Tomato Face watching Silver Bell.

'"They are. All girls are funny," agreed the Grasshopper and giggled at his own observation. "Silver Bell has got a wart on her finger and all. How 'orrible!"

'"Touch her hand and you catch her wart. Ugh!"

'I kept my eye on her wart right on the centre of her ring finger. I thought it was a pretty thing rather than an "'orrible" one.'

'Didn't Silver Bell's dress get terribly wet?' asked Carmina.

'It did but it soon dried in the sun. That night, before going to bed I decided to follow the Pig Man, boots or no boots.'

'And did you?' I wanted to know.

Jesusin did not answer.

'Like every morning, the cockerel woke me at daybreak. I got dressed and made a hat of sorts with a handkerchief that I knotted at the four corners. Then, I slipped out of the house without making any noise.

'To my surprise, I stumbled on a pair of boots that somebody must have left outside the door. There was also a straw hat. Quickly, I exchanged my open sandals for the boots, which were a bit large for me, but I didn't mind. At any moment the sound of the whistle would bring the pigs out to join the Pig Man for their daily forage.'

'Who do you think left those things,' I asked, expecting no reply.

'I thought the boots must have belonged to Tomato Face as he was the biggest of us. The straw hat could have been anybody's, but I would have preferred it to be Silver Bell's.'

'The whistle sounded as the Pig Man appeared from his usual corner. A stampede of pigs ran in his direction and so did I. He gave me a squinty look as if the sun was getting in his eyes. I think he looked sad rather than miserable.

'"Follow me."

'So, off we set for the woods like the Pied Piper taking the rats away from the city, but unlike them, the pigs would return to their homes in the evening with a belly full of acorns.

'The Pig Man did not speak at all. On the way up steep stony paths, he pointed out with his stick the places to avoid, where to tread to avoid a fall. When we reached the thickest part of the wood, we remained there the rest of the day.

'At midday we sat under an oak tree. The Pig Man took out of his shoulder bag a round loaf of bread and an onion and, resting the loaf on his chest, cut several slices. He did the same with the onion.

'You ate bread and onion?' Carmina asked, wrinkling her nose.

Bread and onion! Proper peasant food!

'It tickled my throat a bit and made me pull faces at the beginning, but I soon got used to it.

'The Pig Man grinned. Then, he spoke for the first time.

'"Good for you. Good for farting. Good for burping. OK in the open air. Not at home."

'For a moment the Pig Man's face lost some of its severity. Perhaps he even smiled a little.

'The bread and onion were followed by figs stuffed with hazelnuts. The Pig Man gave me his folding knife and showed me how to slit the figs just enough for a nut to go in.

'"Stuffed figs. Nothing better!"

'He was right. I could eat those all the time.

'After the meal, we moved to a clearing to see the sierra covered in snow, even in the summer.

'"You need a stick. One like mine." The Pig Man took a small branch from a bush and made a stick for me. Then he sat on a rock and carved my name on it.

'"Jesusin," he said, handing it to me.

'While I was enjoying myself in the woods, my friends went to Uncle Timoteo's to invite me to go to the river. They found him very worried over my absence. They soon guessed where I was.

'"Must be with the Pig Man," said Tomato Face.

'"He wanted to go with him," added the Grasshopper.

'"I told him not to go." Silver Bell sounded concerned.

'Uncle Timoteo looked a little happier hearing the news.

'Later in the afternoon I returned home. My uncle was waiting for me and was relieved to see me.

'"Where did you get those boots and hat?"

'"I guess they belong to Tomato Face; the hat must be Silver Bell's."'

His voice changed a bit when he said Silver Bell's name. Carmina wasted no time to giggle in my ear again. 'I told you he's got the shakes for Silver Bell.'

Jesusin sat in the wicker chair as if too tired to continue.

'I need some more of the tonic to give me strength.'

He went out of the room and returned quite a while later with a small glass containing a reddish liquid that he sipped at intervals while he talked. I could not understand some of the things he said because of the big words he occasionally used and his faltering voice but noticed the brightness of tears in his eyes.

'Talking to my friends, I realized that neither the boots nor the hat belonged to them. Besides them, only the Pig Man knew that I wanted to go to the woods.

'After the first trip I accompanied the Pig Man many more times. We became great friends.

'The summer was at an end – the school holidays almost over. Time to return home. Away from the Pig Man. Away from Tomato

Face, the Grasshopper, and, above all, away from Silver Bell. I wished I could take her wart with me. Perhaps what my friends said was true and warts were catching. If I could just hold her hand, if only for a little while, maybe I could catch her wart.

'From that moment on, I made sure to often touch her hand when we were at play. But contrary to what my friends said, there was no sign of Silver Bell's wart on my finger.

Carmina and I were at a loss to understand how he would want to have those unsightly things on his fingers, whether he had the shakes for Silver Bell or not.

'One day, Uncle Timoteo told me about the Pig Man.

'It was a sad story. Almost too sad to mention. The Pig Man's son had died the previous summer. Shortly after his eleventh birthday, he fell down a precipice. The Pig Man could never accept that his son had died.'

I could see tears running down my cousin's face.

'The holiday came to an end. For the last time, I went with the Pig Man to the woods. When we returned, I took off the boots and returned them and the hat to the Pig Man.

'"Thank you." After a few moments of silence, the Pig Man knelt on the ground and hugged me.

'"Goodbye... son."' Jesusin whispered the final words as if they were coming from the Pig Man's lips.

'The following day, about mid-morning, was departure time. Tomato Face and the Grasshopper waved me goodbye from outside the house. No sign of Silver Bell. No sign of Silver Bell's wart on my finger. I was disappointed but not for long. A short distance down the road Silver Bell was also waving goodbye, and for a moment, I felt a strange throbbing on my finger in precisely the same spot where Silver Bell had her wart.'

Jesusin became maudlin as he finished his story. A dreamy look invaded his face. He sat as if drained of energy. Carmina signaled to me that we should go. We spent a few minutes in silence before leaving, though. Then, the rumble of aeroplanes brought Jesusin out of his reverie. The sound of propellers spinning, forcing the metal flyers through the sky, was distinctive.

'They're National planes.' The fear of being bombarded took us by surprise. It was strange for an air raid to take place in the middle of the day. The aeroplanes, four of them, were flying low. We could even see the pilot. No sirens sounded – quite unlike in the night when they hollered announcing a raid. We were huddled together against the balcony doors. I could feel Jesusin trembling.

'They are throwing pieces of paper... leaflets and... and something else,' I pointed out.

'Small sacks,' added Carmina. 'They're coming to liberate us from the Reds!'

Jesusin was more cautious. 'They're sending us food. That's what is in the bags.'

Small bags were landing in the street. Some got caught in the branches of the acacias. People started to appear, approaching the sacks with apprehension.

'Let's go down and see. Quick!' Jesusin commanded.

We ran down the stairs and into the street like lightning. Out of a broken sack several baguettes were showing. We collected several. Most people did the same. But there was also a chorus of discontent.

'The bread could be poisoned. Wouldn't touch it! Those fascists want us dead.'

We were hungry, and in spite of those remarks, the manna from heaven soon found its way to people's flats.

El Militino, with the help of his father and a rickety ladder, climbed an acacia tree and rescued two bags. One contained Vienna rolls. The other, rather heavy, held cans of corned beef.

In hindsight, I cannot but assume that the sirens did not sound because there must have been an agreement on the part of both sides. It was common knowledge what scarcity of food we were suffering.

Boils Galore

'Uncle Fabian has not come to see us for a while,' I told Maria.

'He may not be well after all the persecution he suffered at the hands of those mierdas. Saw cousin Alfonso this morning. Didn't mention anything.'

'He may have had a good reason.'

Maria was concerned. So was I. Alfonso could sometimes be secretive, treating certain things as state secrets. Other times there was no way of stopping him divulging whatever news had caught his fancy.

We were assembling a jigsaw puzzle in a room adjacent to the lounge where our parents were talking. Through the open balcony window we could hear their conversation.

'Fabian is not well. A high temperature is keeping him in bed. He also has a growth in his neck, almost as large as a cherry.'

'A boil?'

'Yes, according to Bonachera.'

'Strange to have a temperature with that!'

'Bonachera says there is a possible infection.'

I could not understand how a boil could ever have cherry proportions.

But Maria knew about high temperature. Fever! She had plenty of it when she went down with enterocolitis.

My father, who must have had some knowledge of first aid, offered to look after the boil and explained to us, as he normally did, the steps to take.

Although we were playing quietly, the shouts of hurrah when the last piece of the puzzle was finally placed broke the silence, alerting my father that we must have heard their conversation. He called us. 'Come in here, the pair of you.'

My father was always diligent in imparting his knowledge – an enjoyable alternative to Doña Amalia's tuition.

'Uncle Fabian is not very well,' he started in his usual kind way.

Then he repeated what we had already heard and enlarged the detail as he went along. My mother listened attentively, and I am sure she wondered whether boils were contagious.

'First you wait until the boil matures; then it must be lanced. After that the pus must be pressed out until the crater is clear. Then comes the cleaning of the crater with oxygenated water (hydrogen peroxide).'

'Is the oxy... water the stuff you put on my knee when I fell?'

'Yes, Manolo, it is the one that bubbles as it evaporates.' My mother was also knowledgeable. I liked the maturing bit. Similar to growing a cherry on the neck. I was not so keen on the lancing, though.

I never saw Uncle Fabian's boil, but I remember that the abating of the fever and final recovery took a long time.

Unfortunately boils came back in different parts of his body. So Doctor Don Juan Bonachera prescribed auto-immunisation. This, I learned later consists in taking blood from a vein and injecting it in the buttocks. I have since learnt that auto-immunization was a useless contribution to medical science and went out of practice in the nineteenth century. The procedure had no effect, curative or otherwise, on Uncle Fabian, who continued to be plagued with boils. Luckily his temperature went back to normal as if his body had become accustomed to the nasty things.

Fulgencio, El Responsable, who was gradually increasing in respect for my father and uncles, expressed his concern about the long period of absence from work.

My father mentioned a conversation relating to the matter.

'Comrade Fabian.' He checked himself. 'Don Fabian is having a rough time. I am responsible for our workers.' He paused, expecting a contribution from my father, who remained silent.

'This Doctor... Bonachera, is he doing his best?'

What Fulgencio wanted to say was 'Is this doctor one of us? Very important that those around him adhered to the regime.

In spite of being reassured that Doctor Don Juan Bonachera had a clean bill of health with the Montero's, he decided to visit the doctor first and Comrade Fabian afterwards, taking with him a large tin of Argentinean corned beef.

Auntie Efigenia, unable to contain her gratitude, kissed both his cheeks, stamping a red lipstick mark on each one.

Fulgencio, a man with marshmallow feelings, showed gratitude on his face. Before parting, with obvious emotion in his heart, Fulgencio shook Fabian's hand and delivered a very important message: 'Doctor will come and see you tomorrow.'

Pepe's Madness

My brothers Pepe and Rafael were bad news.

After the fight with the man who knifed Rafael, Pepe was confined to barracks for a time and subsequently discharged. Because the nitty gritty of the discharge was never made known to the family, my bother's version is the only one I know.

In his own words he played the fool, acting as if he were mental. One day he was found messing about with electricity cables, placing the bare terminals in his mouth. The shock sent him flying across the bay where he was supposed to be working, landing unconscious on the floor with the cables still in his hand. A lieutenant, known for the right handling of new recruits, found him. How my brother was not killed by his stupidity defies belief. He was either lucky or the supply of electricity was at its lowest. At the time, the maximum voltage was only one hundred and ten and it is not unreasonable to imagine that most of the time it was nowhere near that.

In those days, there were not half a dozen psychiatrists to decide whether he was mad or simply playing the fool. Pepe's behaviour could cost dearly. The choices were corporal punishment, time in a military prison, or, more likely, quiet execution. Pepe was lucky, and after a spell in the *calabozo* (military prison cell), resumed ordinary duties. A period of mischief and practical jokes ensued.

He brought his favourite game that he played at home with Rafael to the barracks: the lighting of *fuegos fatuos,* the Spanish version of will-o-the-wisp.

Legend has it, and it may be more than a legend, that at night flames can be seen coming out of graves. Whether this is just a chemical reaction or not I will never know since cemeteries in Madrid and other large cities in Spain are located well away from towns. Not having been in a cemetery late at night, I never came across that experience.

What my brothers referred to as 'fuegos fatuos' was simply the igniting of farts with matches. The best combustible was produced after eating a combination of red beans and cabbage.

The symphony of farts and suppressed giggling could be heard from my bed along with my father's whispering voice. 'Those pigs are at it again.'

Pepe imported the game into the barracks with great success. I am sure enormous hilarity was enjoyed by all.

There were other versions of his mischief.

On one occasion he ran a rope at foot level across the entrance to the dormitory for the purpose of making whoever came trip over. This was designed with the other recruits in mind, but the trick failed and it was the kind lieutenant who hurriedly tripped over the rope. An improvised pirouette kept him vertical. He did not have to think too hard to identify the culprit, and after, what I am sure must have been more than a philosophical admonishment, sent my brother to the calabozo once again.

Pepe, who was hell-bent on getting out of the army, staged a suicide pantomime. He made a noose and stood on a wooden box with it around his neck, keeping his hands free. Not being completely mad and having no intention of dieing, he waited until somebody came into the bay. He waited a long time.

Eventually a recruit came, at which point my brother kicked the box away as he emitted a loud oath. The recruit ran to him, scared out of his wits, and quickly slipped the noose off my brother's neck who continued his charade of screams and oaths. What the recruit did not realize was that there was enough slack in the rope to comfortably stand on the floor.

After this episode, Pepe was confined to the calabozo for his own good and that of every one else. Deliberations over his future between the big chiefs and the kind lieutenant ended quickly. Unanimously. Recruit discharged.

With him back at home, problems restarted. My father decided with the consent of my uncles that a cure for Pepe's antics was hard work that would keep him occupied. In our workshop there was machinery to operate. Uncle Jesus accepted the responsibility of controlling him during the hours of work and training him in the secrets of vertical lathe operating, which was my uncle's forte.

Much to the delight of Fulgencio, Don Salvador's son was to become a manual worker with greasy hands and dark blue dungarees. Real attributes of the proletariat. To crown it all, my brother became Comrade Pepe before he could even think about it. A brief welcome in which words such as 'for the good of the Party', 'unity against the capitalist oppressors', 'forward with the revolution', 'Mother Russia will protect us', and other such niceties, came out of his mouth, fuelled by a passionate heartbeat that said it all.

Pepe was not a happy bunny, and the thought of becoming a vertical lathe operator could not have been further from his thoughts. Uncle Jesus was, on his part, a very unhappy bunny also. My brother managed to disappear from his side with the most unthinkable excuses and, when he was on the machine, purposely ruined the manufacture of a part that was almost ready for delivery. Uncle Jesus hid this in a number of occasions, knowing that my father's patience was reaching a breaking point and that one day he would, inevitably, give Pepe the hiding of his life.

To try a new approach, Uncle Jesus gave Pepe a spell in the garage to inflate pneumatic tyres. A gift from heaven. Inflating tyres? Not enough. Bursting them with excessive pressure was more likely. Nobody could do anything with him, so things continued like a chronic illness continues.

Rafael was a rebel of a different kind, but a rebel all the same. His exploits ranged from tenderness to nastiness. One night in the summer my father discovered three kittens in a very large wardrobe near the entrance door to the flat. I still hear his voice as if things were happening now. He made his way to Rafael's room and said 'Take those cats away before I kill you.'

Rafael and the three kittens made their exit in the dark hours of that very early summer morning. He did not come back that night. The kittens landed over the brick wall in the Red Cross first aid post. Rafael climbed on to the roof and spent the night there.

Funny as this may sound, it was a contravention of discipline and an affront to Michito, the resident cat. I am sure Rafael brought in the kittens for two reasons: one, to give them shelter and two, to annoy our father. That was the essence of his character.

Strange that in families, like in the animal kingdom, there are good and bad eggs from the same progenitors and in the same environment. Amazingly, in my family, with the exception of the two bad eggs, my brothers and sisters were perfectly balanced individuals. Philosophically I have to think about the line 'there but for the grace of God go I'. I do not want to give the impression that I either hated or despised my brothers. I just suffered them the same as everybody else in the family did – a kind of suffering that troubled my life.

El Brasero

Besides the poor supply, we were without electricity for long periods. When coal was no longer available, my mother attempted to cook a few lentils on an *hornillo*, an electric gadget consisting of a metal frame and a *resistance* coiled around some material that had the appearance of clay.

The hornillo did not give any more heat than a slow cooker of today with the disadvantage that the resistance had the bad habit of burning itself out and as a result split into two. When this happened, my brother Salvador twirled the two ends together and heat was restored. I was initiated in this particular science, and, as soon as I became proficient, was put in charge of repairs. Of course the resistance did not last forever.

Trouble. No coal or timber for the kitchen range. Things looked grim. Juanito, hoping to come up with a solution, admitted defeat after taxing his brain to the limit. This surprised the rest of us. El Militino provided an alternative to both electricity and coal.

'My dad has a coke burner. This is where my mum cooks.'

'Coke? What is that?'

'It isn't real coal but looks like it,' El Militino explained.

'It burns with a blue flame and you don't need a chimney.' Juanito knew about coke in detail.

'Is it like the *brasero* (brazier)?' Carlota wanted to know.

Central heating was then an oddity rather than the norm. Electric heaters, ditto. A popular way to keep warm was the brasero. The use of the brasero was not without danger due to the fumes it gave out, especially when the burning embers were not properly handled. It was housed at the foot of a *mesa camilla* (round table fitted with a wooden frame at the bottom to accommodate it). The camilla was covered by a top piece and a skirt made of thick cloth down to the floor. The family would sit around it, legs under the skirt. Having one's legs and lower half warm was normally enough to fend off the cold. When the fumes appeared or when they became noticeably strong, the window had to be opened, to the detriment of the indoor temperature.

There were warning signs, such as a characteristic smell accompanied by a headache. Because of the small enclosure in which the combustion took place, a very small amount of oxygen was necessary. The *tufo*, or fumes, were the dreaded carbon monoxide, which could silently kill. The management of the brasero was normally trusted to the grannies, who acquired experience with age according to Carlota.

We did not have a mesa camilla or a brasero in our flat or a grandmother to manage it. Since I was the tenth child to arrive in this world, there were very few amenities waiting for me. Even in my resigned state of existence, I felt envious of other children when they talked about their grandparents and wondered how different my life would have been if I had arrived first rather than last.

Nobody I knew had a mesa camilla and a brasero, which makes me think those items were relegated to villages or small towns. In our flat its absence was a good thing, as with Pepe's madness alternating between practical jokes and bursts of violence, I would not have put it past him to pour water in it, or worse, to junk the brasero out of its housing and scatter the burning embers all over the place.

The braseros have not been forgotten. An electric version, even fitted with a thermostat, is now in use in some parts of Spain. What people will do to keep up with tradition!

To mitigate our cooking difficulties, El Militino's father came armed with a coke burner, really a small portable stove, for Doña Maria Antonia, as he respectfully referred to my mother. A small bag of coke accompanied the newcomer to the Montero's kitchen and was promptly placed on top of the incumbent kitchen range, sadly out of use.

I was soon instructed in its management. My first assignment was to warm up a saucepan with water in which I diluted a teaspoon of harina sos, a beverage the colour of milk that we acquired from the egg shop from which the eggs had been absent for quite a long time.

With Pepe no longer in the army, gaining safe entry to the stores was not possible. With him as a lookout, Carmina and I, under the watchful eye of Uncle Fabian, had done many sorties in and out of the place.

Food was scarce for everybody, encouraging us to resume our sorties.

Carmina was determined. I was with her. Uncle Fabian, now at least temporarily recovered, saw all manner of difficulties but dismissed them in his own infantile way.

'It's either we die of starvation or we die by the bullet. The end will be the same.' The three of us laughed heartily, our minds not on death but on food.

As usual, we waited till dark and made our way to our destination. We walked in single file, silently. My bravado became thinner with every step we took. I had a heavy feeling in my belly, a kind of premonition. The image of Uncle Fabian hurt by shrapnel on a previous occasion stood vividly before my eyes. I did not want to go any more, and my pace was slowing down all the time. Carmina noticed. She held my hand tightly and we walked together.

'Die of starvation or die by the bullet…' My uncle's words resounded in my ears.

Things were different from the last time. All bushes and scrub that surrounded the stores had disappeared – visibly burnt to extinction. But for a pile of rubble about ten meters from the perimeter fence, there was no hiding place for Uncle Fabian.

'I'll stay here lying down. Nobody will see me. Better than the bushes.' He always made a light predicament from a more difficult one. 'Don't forget I'm here when you come out.' A final smile and Carmina and I made for the fence.

We found our entry hole blocked by barbed wire. Carmina looked at me with determination.

'Must get in, Manolo, we must.'

Darkness was a solid wall. Only our silhouetted surroundings could be made out.

We walked some more round the perimeter. We knew the fence, a chain-link affair, had a few holes along its length. Granted, none of the holes we were familiar with were as safe as the original one. Scaling the fence crowned with barbed wire was no alternative. In our reconnaissance, we walked past a sentry box. A soldier in it was smoking a cigarette. He was joined by another.

'Makes my blood boil.'

'What does?

'That a lot of the food in there will be requisitioned for the families of the big cheeses.'

'The same here. Those bastards are living it up while our comrades are going hungry.'

'It's always so. The big fish takes the lion's share.'

Without saying a word, Carmina pulled me by the hand. We walked quickly towards the soldiers. Carmina started shouting, 'Don't shoot. Don't shoot. We're hungry.' I joined in the shouting.

Time had stopped and we were in front of the soldiers, one of them holding his rifle trained on us.

For a brief moment nobody spoke.

Carmina broke the silence.

'We're hungry. Please give us some food.' Her voice was an almost inaudible whisper and she was crying. A knot formed in my throat. I could not bear to see her cry.

'You come with me, girl.'

'Manolo must come as well,' she pleaded.

'No noise or we will all be shot' was the peremptory warning.

The expected sacks of lentils lined up at the entrance of the stores.

'Can I have some?'

'I'll make a cucurucho with a newspaper and put some in it.' The soldier in his innocence did not expect me to be fully equipped for the operation now in progress.

'They'll go in my pockets.' I showed him how. As the lentils went in, he could not hold back his amazement and burst into a litany of adjectives, which even now I'm not sure have a place in the dictionary.

Carmina was given a round loaf of pan candeal and a tin of corned beef.

The soldier kept looking around for witnesses. With a movement of his hand that encouraged haste, he pointed to the exit, index finger across his lips for silence.

'Don't come back here again. We could have shot you.'

We heard footsteps on the floor above the store and scurried like two cockroaches past the sentry in the box, still smoking. We covered the distance to the pile of rubble where Uncle Fabian was lying immobile on the ground.

'Don't stand up. Crawl behind us.'

Carmina had thought of everything, and once again we made our way home through the deserted streets.

Pepe's Journey

Pepe managed to get a *salvoconducto* (safe-conduct document) to go to Yunquera de Henares, a Guadalajara village only a few kilometres from Madrid. Getting out of Madrid in those days, when the situation was really heating up, was next to impossible. A salvoconducto had to be obtained first, and the circumstances on which it was granted had to be of extreme necessity. But Pepe was cunning if nothing else.

Yunquera was my mother's birthplace. Her whole family: grandparents, brothers, sister, uncles, and aunts were all born and lived there all of their lives. My mother and my Auntie Nativity were the only exceptions who per chance lived in Madrid.

My mother's relatives cultivated the land and owned a factory for the manufacture of bricks, mosaic tiles, pantiles, and the more modest adobes, made from a mixture of clay and mud and baked in the sun.

The purpose of Pepe's visit was to bring potatoes and dried chickpeas home now that the supply of food was almost nonexistent. We were glad to see him go. A few days free from his antics were welcomed by all. He returned with a sack of potatoes and a bag of chickpeas, both harvested by my uncles.

The state of affairs in Yunquera was just as dangerous as in Madrid. And being a small village, where everybody knew everybody else's business, more so. Of course, the favourite target for the Reds was the clergy. This stands to reason, since there was no other target of persecution, with the exception of a few biggish landowners who really had no interest in the revolution and were well-protected by their generosity. Ham, pork, or lamb was never absent from the tables of the higher echelons of society who looked after the needs of the proletariat.

So, Pepe was in his element relating the things he witnessed. Using his characteristic strong imagination, he added details that might not have been quite accurate.

Auntie Petra put him up during his short stay. A middle-aged man shared the house with her. He was the living image of bitterness and was often suffering the effects of too much wine. Auntie Petra, then in her sixties, was a spinster with a sad life story. Twice she had been jilted at the altar, but nobody knew why. When she was young, she was pretty, well-educated, and prosperous.

Pepe took it for granted that the embittered-looking man was her secret lover. This idea was not entirely without logic, since whenever somebody came into the house, he disappeared into an underground *bodeguin* (small wine cellar) the entrance of which was concealed by a board covered with sacks. Once the visitors left, Auntie Petra removed the board, and the embittered man reappeared with the Hessian sack. In spite of his countenance, he was good company, and under the influence, loquacious.

Introductions were made. 'This is Don Tarsicio, my vintner. He takes care of the vines and winemaking. Nobody knows he lives in my house.' She paused. 'You know how malicious people are.' Then she used one of her favourite phrases: 'Least said, soonest mended.' It held an implied message to secure Pepe's silence.

Don Tarsicio overwhelmed Pepe with the science of grape growing and winemaking, explaining how wine matured in wooden casks and was finally bottled and sold. No detail was spared, and a word or two was even added to mention how the profits fattened up her wealth. A visit to the *lagar* (a tread wine press) revealed a rectangular ditch deep enough to accommodate a crop of grapes and wide enough for several barefooted men to stand in to get the juices going.

One day two milicianos armed with rifles called. This was not the only time they had called. Auntie Petra spotted them through the kitchen window, and Don Tarsicio made a quick entry into the bodeguin.

'Where is he'? We heard the unfriendly greeting given by the milicianos.

'This is my nephew, Pepe. He's here with me for a few days. He comes from Madrid.'

'Salvoconducto,' they demanded. They scrutinized the bit of paper out of my brother's pocket and then returned it without a comment.

Auntie Petra's evasion enraged the men. 'Where's that fucking priest? We know you're hiding him here, and we'll find him even if we have to set the house on fire. We'll burn the bastard to death, and you with him, you bloody old witch.'

The milicianos took turns barking threats. They carried out a search of the ground floor. They thumped every inch of the wooden floor with their rifle butts. The entrance to the bodeguin returned a hollow sound. The pair trained a murderous look on Auntie Petra and Pepe.

'That's the bodeguin. Casks and bottles are kept there.'

They removed the board and viewed what was described by my aunt. We allowed ourselves a momentary sigh of relief. Then the milicianos laughed with sarcasm. They said, 'Those casks are large enough to hide a whole monastery.'

The milicianos went down into the bodeguin and knocked on every cask until they found the one where their prey was hiding.

'Get out of there, you bastard.'

Don Tarsicio came out of the barrel and exploded into a semi-incoherent rage. He said, 'I spend my life in the service of the Lord, and what do I get: nothing but persecution and threats. Well I tell you that if this is the way God rewards me, *que le den por culo* (bugger Him) *porque yo estoy hasta los cojones* (I'm up to my balls) with this religion, *cabrona* (bastard). *Me paso mi vida sin follar* (I spent my life without a fuck), and all I get is promises after death. Now you know what I think of God, *la puta virgen*, the bloody host, and all the other lies…'

He continued in this vein till his throat ran dry. The milicianos laughed loudly at his performance. In spite of the bitterness in which it was delivered, he showed a comical side to desperation. They realized that they came to apprehend a priest, and now they were dealing with a defenceless madman instead. The trio came up and joined Auntie Petra and Pepe.

So, Don Tarsicio was not a vintner but a priest in hiding. I can imagine my aunt and brother witnessing this performance with incredulous ears.

'Don't think that your performance is going to save you. You're coming with us to be interrogated,' said one of the men.

'And soon after, you'll join your Maker, *su puta madre* (His mother the whore), and the rest of them up in heaven or down in hell.' The miliciano laughed at his peroration.

'This's how I feel,' Don Tarsicio clarified bitterly. At this point, Don Tarsicio was purple in the face, his eyes revealed anger, and he was frothing at the mouth with rage. Pepe expected him to throw himself at them like a corralled animal. I am sure my brother would have followed suit if that had happened. Instead, Don Tarsicio suddenly stopped ranting, and, doing the sign of the cross, said, 'Jesus

Christ, forgive me,' as he stared towards the ceiling. Then, resigned, he said, 'take me to the tribunal. I'm prepared to die.' There was a brief pause, and then he said, 'I must take my crucifix with me.'

'Take it. Take it. The tribunal will be impressed,' said one of the milicianos with derision.

'It will be a nail in your coffin, guaranteed', mocked the other.

Don Tarsicio turned round, and from a box on top of a tall sideboard pulled out a rather large 'crucifix'. He fired a shot. One of the milicianos fell dead on the floor.

'This is the best crucifix I ever possessed,' Don Tarsicio said sarcastically as he pointed a revolver at the other miliciano. As for you, *piojo* (louse), you'd better kneel down in front of your priest for confession.' Panic showed in the miliciano's face. 'You can now confess your sins,' Don Tarsicio said, and, watching the fear on the man's face, tightened up the screw a little. 'All of them.'

The miliciano started to divulge his sins. It was clear the man felt genuine contrition. 'Let me kick his cojones before this pig dies,' Pepe requested, but it was not granted.

Don Tarsicio's revolver was trained on the kneeling louse's head the whole time. Then he spoke, sounding as if he were officiating mass, he said, 'Die per Christus Domine nostrum.' He fired another shot, and the second miliciano was dead.

Immediately Don Tarsicio turned the revolver to his temple and squeezed the trigger. A metallic click followed, then another, and another. He threw the revolver away and knelt on the floor for a silent prayer. Auntie Petra whispered the word *miracle* many times. So did Pepe once he realized that was the correct thing to do.

Don Tarsicio, who had faced the barrel of a gun countless times, recovered quickly. He said, 'These two were simply carrying out somebody else's orders. They deserve a proper grave. It's not their fault that they were working for the wrong cause.'

Don Tarsicio and Pepe carried the bodies and weapons and dumped them in the lagar. A load of straw and mud destined for making adobe covered the bodies.

Not everybody in the family believed Pepe's narration of this story, at least not in total. But years after the civil war finished and the dust of past events had settled in many people's memory, Auntie Petra confirmed the facts to my mother in rather a subtle way. 'We don't make wine anymore,' she said to my mother during a later visit we made to Yunquera. 'The lagar has been used for another purpose.'

Stages of Tragedy

Events were relatively quiet for a while. But the drip, drip of tragedy never ceased.

Jesusin, in spite of the "powerful" Fowler's solution, was not showing signs of improvement. On the contrary, as the intake of arsenic continued, his condition deteriorated. A visit to Doctor Don Juan Bonachera was indicated.

The doctor shook his head when he saw his patient. Not only did he look as skeletal as ever, but also his skin showed brownish, flaky patches.

'He was vomiting all day yesterday.' Auntie Ignacia informed Doctor Bonachera. 'Also, he feels dizzy.'

Stethoscope at the ready, the doctor listened to Jesusin's chest and heart, took his pulse, and prodded his belly. The doctor was pensive. Then he said, 'We'll need to increase the number of drops to twenty for a few days.'

My cousin looked at him, knowing too well that he had ignored the doctor's instructions and opted for his own dosage of the medicine. 'I'm already on thirty-five,' he said sheepishly.

Doctor Bonachera turned purple. 'In that case,' he said, addressing Auntie Ignacia, 'we will stop the drops altogether. We are dealing with arsenic. Too much of it could result in many disorders or even death.'

Auntie Ignacia listened to the news with resignation, in particular to the self-medicating overdose by her son. Had it not been for his frailty, she would have administered one of her favourite slaps across his bum.

Uncle Jesus had words to say to his son on his return home. Uncle Jesus recommended cautious consideration of his foolishness. While he spoke, his handlebar moustache became alive under his nose.

Above my uncle's second-floor flat, on the third floor, lived Doña Encarnacion, owner of the property. She was a well-dressed woman in her sixties who represented simple elegance. She lived alone until shortly before the arsenic episode. Then, either due to her own volition or because it was imposed by the regime, three adults and a child came to live with her. It was understood that in times of stress, when so many buildings were either demolished or uninhabitable, those with room in their houses should take in the homeless.

Jesusin complained, 'Since those four arrived, there has not been a moment's peace. It is as if an earthquake is about to strike. That horrible child runs his tricycle all over the place, and the other three do nothing but shout at Doña Encarnacion all the time.' He conveyed not only his thoughts, but also those of his mother.

Often Doña Encarnacion would appear on the balcony to address neighbours and passersby. She said, 'I want everybody to hear me. I gave shelter to this family, and they repaid me destroying my home. Somebody help me. Take away from here these disgusting people before I kill myself.' These public addresses did not fall on deaf ears. But how could anybody help? There was a background chorus of mockery and insults by the three "disgusting people". Luckily, the child was not allowed to join in. He tried once, to his misfortune, and was silenced with a sonorous, disciplining slap across his face.

On the first floor of the block lived a professor of veterinary medicine. He was a nice man as I remember. He was totally non-political in his career and his life. His son, Emiliano, was a different kettle of fish. From the beginning of the war, he had imbibed the communistic ideas with a high degree of concentration. He was another individual who abided by the tune that Russia would defend us. It was a stock phrase he used when nothing better came to mind. Having listened to many an address by Doña Encarnacion, he went to see her one day, but not to help.

He went to acquaint her with the need of all of us to pull together for the triumph of the party. It was her duty to accommodate the people the authorities had put under her shelter. So that was it. We learned for sure the quartet was imposed by the authorities. Emiliano wasted no time in divulging the news around the neighbourhood. His quest to help was brief and the effect on her attitude unknown.

Doña Encarnacion's addresses continued, but there were some periods of calm. There was a truce perhaps. But, as is not unusual in human behaviour, her belligerency resumed. At times we heard the sound of utensils flying inside the kitchen and saw them fly out into the street.

The snipers continued to break the night silence. It was strange that no sniper was ever caught. One morning, the body of a woman was found on the pavement. There was a stick near her skirt stained with coagulated blood. I did not see the horrible figure. Maria heard screams in the night. Was it a nightmare? The body was removed as life started to populate the street. The body was removed, but the bloodstains remained. Groups formed nearby. Gestures of despair, resignation, and hate created a melange of feelings. Somebody recognised the body as that of a nun.

An unidentified voice from the crowd was heard. 'One more clerical parasite exterminated. Down with the *curas* (priests) and *monjas* (nuns). Eradicate the vermin.'

It was a resolute expression of the Reds. Groups dispersed silently. In the situation, one never knew who their friends were. It was a prerogative of all civil wars. Showing your feelings could cost dearly. So we went from one tragedy to another. It was a Russian roulette staged by circumstances.

Jesusin's vomiting and dizziness did not stop. A fit shook his body so violently that he fainted. Even then the convulsions did not stop. Auntie Ignacia applied a bottle of smelling salts to his nose in an attempt to get him to regain consciousness. This bottle of salts was used in past occasions with success, but not so this time. The salts had become a gelatinous gel. She kept the bottle at his nose to no avail. Eventually the convulsions ceased. His breathing changed intermittently between normal and difficult. After a while, he went to sleep and woke up to blindness. I can still hear the horror in my aunt's voice when she told my mother.

Jesusin completely lost the sight in his left eye. With the right one, he could just perceive changes in light. He could tell when the sun shone and when the clouds covered it. His corneas became opaque, like if he had milk glass stuck to the front of his eyes.

An ophthalmologist at the Red Cross centre examined him, prescribed drops, and gave him hope. But it was hope that would take a long time to be fulfilled. Surprisingly, Jesusin did not succumb to his tragedy. He decided to come back from the ashes. He wanted to paint like he had always done. With the advice of the Ophthalmologist, Uncle Jesus made him an eye piece. It was a small sheet of Bakelite fashioned into a circle and a short handle. A pinhole was bored into the circular part of the gadget.

'The pinhole is for the purpose of concentrating light and the residual vision available,' explained the Ophthalmologist. He was right.

Carmina and I went to keep Jesusin company. He was over the moon about the device. 'Look,' he said as he sat at a small table in his room, 'see how this works. I can read words looking through this hole.' He held the eyepiece to his right eye and read a few words from a book. 'I can also draw.' Now he held the eyepiece with his left hand while with the other sketched the silhouette of a bird. 'Of course, I cannot move about with this thing in front of my eye, but I can see things when I'm sitting.'

Then there was a silence that could be translated into a mixture of doubt and hope. The Ophthal says I'm going to improve,' he said. His voice had lost some of its zest.

Auntie Ignacia blamed herself for his condition. Her mood was taciturn with guilt. But no one in the family saw the situation as being her fault. The salts were the only things available, and when she saw her son at death's door, she hoped they would bring him back. And they would probably have achieved their purpose had they not been in a state of decomposition that scorched the corneas.

The White Wolf

Don Ricardo, who was very fond of Jesusin, was badly shaken when he heard the news. He said, 'Carmina, ask Doña Ignacia if Jesusin would like to come and spend a little while with us. We could read him a story, or better still, I could tell him about my journeys around the country.'

Don Ricardo was a technical inspector for the railways. It was work that entailed much travelling. When something went wrong, off he went to the troubled spot.

Jesusin was delighted to come. His eyepiece was well-ensconced in his shirt pocket, and Carmina was his *lazarillo* (guide).

Doña Carmen prepared two small Vienna rolls, buttered and sprinkled with sugar. There was a whole roll for my cousin and half of the other roll apiece for Carmina and myself.

'I'm going to tell you about my journey to Reinosa in the middle of the winter,' Don Ricardo said.

'Reinosa. Is it far away?' Jesusin asked.

'Very. It is a village near Santander in the north of Spain. It is so far that the train journey from Madrid took all night. That was the Express. Had it been the *correo* (mail train) that stops at every station, it would have taken even longer. The compartment was packed, every seat taken. Also, people were sitting on the floor. In this train, unlike those which run during the day, there were no peddlers, entertainers, or people doing raffles. So we all went to sleep, and soon snoring echoed along with the continuous noise of the train, kilometre after kilometre.

By daybreak we were well up north travelling through snow-covered fields. We enjoyed a beautiful view from the warmth of the steam giant that was puffing clouds of smoke.'

'And *carbonilla* (specs of coal dust),' Jesusin added.

'Yes. There's always some carbonilla when the locomotive puffs out smoke, especially when the smoke is black.'

'A bit of carbonilla in your eye. That's nasty!' my cousin said, wiping his eye, as if to disperse the cloud that permanently obscured his vision.

Don Ricardo continued, 'We arrived midmorning. It was later than expected due to blizzards. The weather was so bad that, within a day, the village became cut off from the surrounding countryside. This happens every year. Deep snow makes it impossible to get in or out of Reinosa. Food runs short. The snow creates a kind of blockade that can last from days to weeks.'

'Blizzards? What are blizzards?' I asked.

'They are strong winds that blow bits of snow as they come down, icy and blinding, Manolo. Everything looks white. Icicles hung from the edges of roofs and remain there the whole winter. There is a legend that a white wolf...'

I was not taking much notice of what Don Ricardo was saying. His voice droned in my ears. My mind was occupied with my mother's toothache, which for a few days had become constant. No matter how many cloves she put on the tooth responsible for the pain or how many Our Fathers she prayed to the very popular San Antonio de Padua, the pain would not go away. A visit to the *sacamuelas* (tooth puller, dentist) was a dreadful thought that she fought to exhaustion. But pressure and cajoling from my older siblings caused her to succumb.

Sacamuelas Aragon, a brother of Señor Aragon de Pharmacist, had his clinic the opposite corner of General Oraa y Castello. It was close enough for Maria and me to see into it. That was where everything happened. My mother decided to put her teeth in his hands and selected the two of us to accompany her. Before going, Maria told me that Sacamuelas Aragon had only one-and-a-half ears, as part of one was fatally singed by an exploding container of chemicals that caught fire. From our balconies, we could actually see the black evidence that the fire imprinted on the façade of the building.

Sacamuelas Aragon was a thin and amiable man who worked on his own according to the fashion of the time. He could, however, summon his wife's help, when the use of force was deemed necessary for those cases where the patient had to be held down on the chair.

The smell of disinfectant mingled with other unidentified smells unleashed all manner of fear in my belly. In spite of that, I surveyed the room, the equipment, and his modus operandi.

He had no high-speed electronic drills then. He just had a foot operated one; he pedaled as the drill bit excavated the teeth. There were no state-of the-art-lights either, just an ordinary bulb sheltered by a green shade. There was no running water to be seen, just a jug showing the scars of time. There was also a white vitreous spittoon with a hole in the middle that drained into an open bucket for discarded mouth fluids.

I assume anesthetic was used for women only. Men did not need any. Pain was nothing to a man. Only a sissy would request anesthetic.

My mother gave Sacamuelas Aragon a pleading look that said it all. The dentist's chair was not for her, and she insisted on holding Maria's hand during the duration of the expected ordeal. That day, my mother was not in luck, and as soon as the drilling commenced, the skies opened with fierce torrential rain followed by tremendous thunder. Lightning flashed bluish lights that, together with the tooth excavation, made my mother feel that the day of reckoning had arrived. All-in-all, we lived to tell the tale, and Maria and I returned home with a much happier mother than she had been for some days.

I re-focused on what Don Ricardo was saying. He continued, '...So I went with a team of men to the troubled spot, walking on the channels made in the snow, which was well above our knees. We set out under a clear sky without a trace of bad weather. We walked fast on an embankment that ran alongside the railway line. Unexpectedly, the weather turned bad. The wind started to blow soon and gained strength. "A snowstorm is brewing," said one of the men. "There's no point to continuing," said another.

'In the distance, the village was gradually being enveloped in a milky sort of veil. In next to no time, we found ourselves in the middle of a severe blizzard.'

My thoughts were now on the white wolf. I forced myself to listen. It was difficult when Don Ricardo was using too many grown-up words.

'Was there a white wolf?' I was impatient to know.

'Things got so bad we decided to return to Reinosa. Even in the middle of the day, we found it difficult to see because of the blinding wind, and we became disorientated. We stood still, forming a small circle to protect ourselves from the biting wind in the hope that the adverse conditions would clear. But that did not happen.

'I do not remember how long we were there, frozen to the marrow. But I remember the howling of a wolf in the distance as clearly as I did when I was there in the centre of the blizzard. The howling became louder and louder.

"That's Whity. I know it is," said one of the men. 'According to a legend, there is an old white wolf that on stormy days seeks the company of people and walks with them to the outskirts of Reinosa'.

'Have you ever seen it?' I asked him. Don Ricardo wanted to know.

'I have. Many times… and given him food.' He spoke as if talking about an old friend.

'Soon the howling stopped. The sound of hooves followed. Then Whity appeared. It was a magnificent wolf covered in mostly white fur.'

'Were you not scared, dad?'

'I would have been. Wolves have sharp teeth,' Jesusin said. He knew about wolves' teeth.

'I'd like to have seen it.'

'And you would have liked it, Manolo.'

'We did not have much food between us, but we managed to rustle some up for him.'

'Is it true that Whity would come with you to Reinosa,' I asked. The three of us all wanted to know the answer.

'Yes, but only to the outskirts. There Whity turned around. We watched him till he disappeared from sight.'

Adversity

Autumn marched into winter with gigantic steps, a climatic trait of the Madrid weather. Days of rain gave way to frost, ice, and subsequent snow. But the snow was never abundant; it was simply treacherous enough to spread a thin cover that turned into ice and remained frozen for days. This must have affected the water supply, leaving many blocks without running water.

There were two main suppliers: Canales Lozoya and Santillana. We belonged to the former. It was the best water, crystalline and clean. Santillana, which supplied many blocks in the vicinity, was bad news. They provided water with a certain greyish hue, a peculiar odour, silty sediment, and an earthy taste.

But this day, whatever the quality of the water and whatever the reason, the pipes were dry. As usual, rumours started to circulate. Some blamed the cold weather. Others floated the theory of sabotage.

'It's the fascists. They've gone and cut the water to make us die of thirst,' one neighbour said.

Somebody disagreed. 'They would not cut the water. It's too smart for them. They'll poison it is more like it.'

The first responded, 'Sure as I'm alive, they've done this. Death to all of them.'

Maria and I could hear their voices, which sounded more like grunts from behind the balcony window. I did not understand what they were saying. But the meaning was clear. There were some very angry people in the street. I'm sure my sister understood every word. Her face showed fear like there was a brewing storm.

The protesting group grew in numbers, and like a flock of starlings with no identified leader, it went in the direction of Principe de Vergara. The final destination was unknown to us.

Carmina came down with the news that a shop in Lagasca Street, only about fifteen minutes away, had eggs for sale. This was a commodity not to be passed up. So she, together with Maria, equipped themselves with *hule* bags and went on their way. I kept a watch on the egg scouts sliding about on the ice until they disappeared from sight.

Hule was a waterproof material. In all probability, it was rubberised or oil cloth—perhaps a very early predecessor of plastic. The bags were small and black. They were just big enough for a loaf of bread or a kilo of potatoes. Some lettering in dull red makes me think they were given as a freebee for advertising. They could well have been from Montero Hermanos S.A. to advertise a product connected with the industry.

My mother had been born and grew up till the age of about twenty in Yunquera de Henares, Guadalajara. It was in essence an agricultural little village. In our view, she had never forgotten her peasant roots. 'We always had plenty of water,' she told my brother Salvador. 'We just went to the Four Jets fountain with our pitchers and brought the water home.'

In my mother's younger days, there was no running water in the houses. No toilets existed. Therefore, the need to flush the cistern did not occur. People lived in a different way. What they never had, they did not miss. The same situation prevailed for many years. I experienced it when I was about six. Having to go to the corral to relieve myself was a game I would have preferred not to play.

Salvador and the rest of us were tolerant of our mother's ideas. On this occasion, he found inspiration in what she said. Mobilising Pepe and Rafael, they took some old cans and empty bottles and made their way to the nearest waterhole, El Canalillo.

The idea was not exclusive to my eldest brother. A crowd was already hard at work doing the same thing when they arrived. Cans and bottles were filled. Not a drop was spilled. And the three of them returned home to a heroes' welcome from a satisfied mother.

Maria and Carmina got back a while after my brothers. Carmina had six whole eggs in her hule bag. Maria had six broken ones, ready for an omelette. The eggs were victims of a fall. It was omelette time. The problem was what to put in it. Some potato peel left over from a previous meal, wrapped in a newspaper sheet. *Oro en Paño* (A gold treasure)!

I wondered how the pigeons would fare in the cold weather. Carlota and I went to see Don Cesar. We found him on the rooftop, well-wrapped in a heavy coat, a hat that covered his ears, and with one gloved hand. The free hand was distributing the feed. He was purposely dropping some around his feet to feel the nearness of the birds.

The floor made of red quarry tiles glistened in the sun—an anaemic sun that hardly melted the ice that coated everything. Flowerpots showing a white dome of snow resembled confectionery soufflés.

Don Cesar was happy to see us. 'Be careful,' he said. 'The floor is very slippery.'

It was too late of a warning. Carlota had already landed on her behind. She laughed. We all did.

'Don't the pigeons feel the cold?' she asked.

'They don't seem to mind very much.'

I noticed their little legs. They were as red as Don Cesar's nose. Marina came to the door.

'Come in out of the cold, the three of you, before you catch pneumonia,' she said.

We obeyed.

Don Cesar had a pained expression on his face and at times he uttered a slight moan. Later I learnt from Carmina that his side had been giving him trouble. She said, 'Doña Marina and I are going with him to the Red Cross tomorrow to see the doctor. You can come as well.' I did.

The temperature rose in a few days, allowing the water to flow again. It was not the fascists after all that caused the difficulties.

The rumble of gunfire had been serenading us since early morning. It made a nasty background noise. We heard different tones of the same thing and the rat-a-tat of the machine guns repeating itself. It was only muffled by the basso profundo boom of a cannon. The sporadic bursting of hand grenades reduced targets to bits amidst showers of shrapnel and dust. We could not see any of that from where we were; we could only hear it. And that brought to mind scenes that the four of us had already witnessed.

The four of us: Don Cesar, Doña Marina, Carmina, and I on our way to the Red Cross went down General Oraa and made a right turn at Nuñez de Balboa where the entrance was.

It was difficult to know how distant the shooting was.

'It must be far away,' Don Cesar reassured us.

In spite of that, we felt unsettled. There was no conviction in his words.

'The doctor has given him a box of pills and a box of ampoules,' Carmina told me in a low voice.

I knew what pills were. Ampoules were uncharted territory for me. When I grew up, Rafael told me that Don Cesar was a morphine addict. Morphine was prescribed for kidney pain that can be very severe, but he faked it.

When we came out of the Red Cross, the battle noise had increased, and it continued to do so. We could now see the shooting coming from the fields beyond Maria de Molina. Soon, open lorries with milicianos came into view.

We quickened our pace and then had a moment of hesitation. Should we retrace our footsteps and go back into the Red Cross post for safety? Perhaps it would be best to run to the corner of General Oraa. I had a sudden thought: There was nothing in that part of our street for the milicianos to target.

'The milicianos won't come up towards Castello,' Don Cesar said, almost out of breath. How wrong he was. They did not need to. The target was right there near the intersection of the streets.

Two lorries unloaded their cargo on the very corner blocking the crossing. The milicianos took their positions. Machine guns and rifles started to spit. The place under attack was the old photographic studio, now burnt out after the famous fire. A hand grenade joined in the spray of bullets. Doña Marina was trembling so much she fell on the ground. Her legs would not hold her.

'Get down. Get down,' Don Cesar said with a faltering voice.

'Down, Manolo, down. Get down.' Carmina pulled me down and covered me with her arms.

A second hand grenade was thrown. There was a deafening explosion, a thud, a splash of blood landed on my face. And Carmina was dead.

The Last Farewell

I do not want to remember that day or the days that followed. But the memory is indelible; it's imprinted on my mind forever.

I don't know how long we were in the street embracing its hard surface. How long Carmina's blood trickled on my face, finding its way to my mouth, is now in the realm of confusion. How loud Doña Marina whimpered and cried, I know not. The image of Don Cesar kneeling next to me, holding Carmina's body in his arms and roaring with the agony of sadness, has remained with me as hauntingly fresh as when it happened.

For what seemed a never-ending episode, one explosion followed another without the need of bullets or hand grenades. The old photographic site must have been used for storing ammunition by a dissenting faction, of which there were several. That explained the attack. There was nobody on the site, and therefore there were no deaths on the site. No, death was on the hard pavement.

Someone came with a stretcher from the Red Cross post. The rest of us followed, with help. Doña Marina had to be carried. Don Cesar and I walked. My hair was matted, and one side of my face was caked with drying blood. I will never be sure if the pavement waved under my feet. The sky, so far clear, had taken a dark tone, like when night is on its way. But I could perceive the flashing of intermittent brightness against the sudden darkness. I could hardly see out of my right eye because my eyelid was stuck with coagulated blood. Suddenly dizziness took over, and I must have fallen unconscious. When I woke, I found myself in the hands of first-aid workers. My head had been shaved, showing a deep gash across the skull that was still bleeding.

A doctor came. He said, 'I'm going to stitch that cut in your head,' then, he said something humorous. I chose not to hear it. He proceeded with the stitching. I felt no pain. I was beyond that.

A bandage was put round my head, and I was sent home to my mother, who was in belligerent conflict with San Antonio de Padua; my violent brothers; and my sister Amelia, who always ranted due to her psychological deficiency and the hate between her and Pepe that resulted in never-ending shouting matches and often came to physical violence. And she screamed in the night when nightmares struck.

I went home to my sister Martina, who tried to bring harmony into the house; to my father, who made supreme efforts in order not to go under financially; to Maria, for whom the tragedy that surrounded us was more real than for myself; and to my eldest brother, coughing blood as a harbinger of tuberculosis.

I was so immersed in sadness that my head wound hardly mattered. The fear of suffering violence by my brothers did. It was a feeling that unsettled me then and for many years to come. Amidst all that, Uncle Fabian's mantra echoed in my ears. 'One day, this war will end…' Yes. One day when it is all too late.

I spent a lot of time with Carlota in Ali Baba's cave. We sat together on the cushions she had embroidered. Our heads touched as we bent over *Arabian Nights*. One of us interrupted our reading to wipe a furtive tear. I often felt a shudder of panic in my stomach at the thought that Carlota could come to a tragic end.

My mother and sisters went to keep company with Doña Carmen, Don Ricardo, and her big brother, Ricardo, back from the trenches for the funeral. It was a last farewell. I did not have the courage to go with them. A heavy feeling stayed around my waking hours and my sleep. There would be no more ludo, no more listening to the Pilot radio, and no more would we sit round the table to make paper ships, hats, or kites. All that was now gone. Perhaps in time, the women would get together to knit sweaters and socks for the soldiers. But Carmina will not be there.

Septicaemia

It must have been months that Uncle Fabian suffered from carbuncles on and off. But at long last he recovered. Fulgencio welcomed him with open arms as a father would the return of a prodigal son.

Small scars remained on his skin as a reminder.

Because we went from one problem to another, it was now my father whose health was at a stake. He started to develop a boil on his neck in a similar place that my uncle had. The boil grew steadily and became more painful as it developed. The shirt collar rubbing on that part of the neck irritated the skin. He had to wear a silk scarf to try and mitigate the discomfort. Doctor Coronel spotted it when they both converged in the entrance hall of the block, and he knew about my uncle's history.

Their encounter must have gone something like this:

'Sore throat?' he asked my father.

'A boil. It's giving me hell.'

'Perhaps I ought to have a look at it, Salvador.'

Dr. Coronel was not only a caring man, he was also a good friend of the family, and because he lived in an upstairs flat, he was easy to reach.

He explained to my father the nature of boils, even though my father had already experienced them when treating my uncle. Nevertheless, Dr. Coronel deemed this to be the opportunity to briefly explain how these nasty eruptions form. Infection takes place at the root of one or more hair follicles, and bacteria are the culprit. The skin turns red. Lumps appear and quickly fill with pus, growing larger and more painful until they rupture. The pus then flows out.

A carbuncle is a far more serious thing. It is a cluster of boils that can cause a deeper and more severe infection than boils. Now I know that carbuncles can appear rather suddenly as a result of a weak immune system from tiredness, poor nutrition, causing a fever and even perhaps a chill.

Dr. Coronel said, 'I'd like to look at this more in detail, Salvador. You've been applying your bother's treatments, and the risk of contagion is high. Any trace of pus or fluid when the thing bursts could find its way onto your hands and infect you.' Doctor Coronel volunteered to treat my father. He applied a compress soaked in warm, salty water several times a day. Because of this frequency, my mother was also involved in the treatments. After the compress treatment, the carbuncle was dabbed with pungent-smelling oil. I assume it was tea tree oil.

Unfortunately, the treatment did not have much effect. My father developed a high fever and was confined to bed. I remember him shivering under the bedclothes with added blankets and a hot water bottle. In better times, the bottle had contained wine. Most of the time my father was delirious, and when this was not so, he was choking with pain and asking for God's mercy. His condition deteriorated quickly.

The carbuncle seemed to have burst and dried, but the infection had already gone into the blood. A different doctor took over from Doctor Coronel and prescribed daily injections. I was never able to find out what the injections were. A *practicante* (male nurse) came every day to deal with the injections and to do something else. My father was unable to pass urine regularly, so that had to be extracted with a *sonda urinaria* (a non-permanent catheter). El practicante showed my brother Salvador how to do this. The procedure had to be carried out a couple of times a day.

Because of the severity of his condition, my father was moved from the marital bed to another bed larger than a single one but not quite as large as a double bed. (The Spanish term to define this size bed is a body-and-a-half bed.)

I wonder how he must have felt departing from the marital bed, which was a metal structure with golden vertical bars joining the top and bottom of the frame. In this bed, all my brothers and sisters were born. I was the only one who broke the tradition and came to this world in a maternity clinic. But, not wanting to be left out of the tradition, I climbed many times to the top of the foot end with the help of the golden bars that I considered magic.

The new doctor added a new word to the grown-ups' conversations: septicaemia, also known as blood poisoning. The infection had found its way to the blood. This was very bad news.

My mother ceased to pray to San Antonio de Padua or even to mention his name. Instead she faced the stark reality with great courage. One of us was always at my father's bedside, day and night. Pepe was excluded for obvious reasons. Amelia stayed with him only for short periods due to her very poor hearing.

The day of Los Reyes Magos (the three Wise Men), the sixth of January, was approaching. I was sitting by his bed one evening. There was very little light in the room, and I could just about make out the shape of his body. His fast and laboured breathing, together with his constant pleading for mercy, conjured up an eerie ambiance.

'Who's there?' he whispered, gasping for air.

'It's me, Dad. Manolo.'

He was silent for a while as if trying to regain enough sense to speak.

'Have you written a letter to Los Reyes Magos?'

A knot came to my throat.

'Yes, Dad, I have.'

There was another pause. This time it was a much longer one.

'What did you ask for?'

'That Daddy gets well.'

My sister Martina relieved me to take another night shift in the chair close to his bed.

Eating became a problem. Solid foods were out. Only liquids such as soups or ones somewhat thicker like liquidy mashed potatoes were administered. Martina and my mother fed him tiny amounts at a time with a teaspoon. After a while, feeding had to be done with a *pistero* (earthenware with a longish spout).

The degree of deterioration continued to mount, with a spiking fever, a rapid heartbeat, and a falling temperature, just to mention a few of the effects of the disease. One morning, in desperation, my father made a superhuman effort to get up. He had to go to work. This would make him better. He wanted no more staying in bed and no more injections. In a semi-delirious state, he pushed the bedclothes to one side and sat on the edge, ready to get dressed. My brother Salvador was with him. and tried desperately to dissuade him and get back under the covers. My father was in shock: trembling, regurgitating saliva, and having extreme convulsions. His body temperature must have fallen to the lowest limit. My mother and Martina came to help, and between the three of them they managed to get him back in bed and rearrange the bedclothes. During his ordeal, my father kept on saying something, most of it unintelligible. Doctor Coronel was called. He gave my father an injection. Then my father slept, but it was not a relaxed sleep.

My father suffered confusion for days to come. He was in a semi-permanent delirious estate. No more asking for mercy. His words now were, 'pen... pen. Sign document... El tarjeton.'

None of us knew the meaning of *el tarjeton*. But it was not difficult to understand what 'pen,' and 'sign document' meant. He knew he was at death's door and wished to make his testament.

Bullets of Death

To help Don Cesar with his bad back, Carlota and I went to the terrace every day to feed the pigeons and to replenish their drinking water. There were several shallow clay vessels, which we cleaned and filled up. There were also some deeper ones for the birds to bathe in. In warm summer days, we enjoyed watching the birds' routine of immersion. It was rather comical how they dipped their wings and dunked their whole bodies in the water. After a few ablutions, a good shake dispersed the droplets. Lying in the sun followed. It was a show that Carlota and I would not miss for the world.

Like Don Cesar showed us, we sprinkled the feed close to our feet to feel the contact of the feathers on our legs. We were given a *real* (small coin with a whole in the middle) each for our labour. Mine was always destined to finance a liquorice bar and some aniseed twists. Carlota saved hers to buy a doll. She threaded the coin through a gap in an old *botijo* (earthenware water cooler). Once the money was entrusted to it, it remained there until the botijo was broken. My friend judged the extent of her bounty by the increase in weight, like fattening a pig!

This day, our task finished, we went to Ali Baba's cave for a read.

'On Sunday, my parents are going to take me to El Retiro (Madrid's Park). My auntie Sophie will come as well.' She giggled when she mentioned her auntie Sophie. 'She looks like an owl... her nose is ever so long and curves right over her lip, just like an owl's nose. And she wears glasses that keep on sliding down her nose all the time.'

'I wish I could see her,' I said.

'You will. I'll draw her face for you.' She took a piece of paper from a scribbling pad and a crayon and started doing a sketch.

She worked on it for a while. Auntie Sophie's face was as she had described it but for the nose, which looked more like an overripe carrot. I pulled her leg.

'I ran out of the right crayon, Manolo. I'll finish it when I come back.'

We had a good laugh.

'Doña Maria Antonia has given me *alpiste* (bird feed) for the birds. She said there are plenty in El Retiro.'

'Doña Maria Antonia?' I was puzzled.

'I know she's your mum, but I like to call her Doña Maria Antonia. It's such a lovely name.'

'I was with her earlier and watched La Chugue catch a cockroach. It was so funny.'

'I'm so glad your mum likes me now. She even gave me a kiss and said to come back and tell her about our day in El Retiro.'

Hearing this encouraged me to believe in miracles.

On Monday, Carlota did not come to school.

'She's been kidnapped by her owlish aunt,' El Militino said as he pulled a face to match the description.

'Worse luck. She may have been caught by the fascists.' Juanito thought that was a more likely story.

But, in spite of our surprised giggles, the three of us missed her.

'You can go and see what she's up to.' I was detailed with the task.

There was no reply when I rang Carlota's bell. As usual, when this happened, I composed a letter. It was a secret plot the two of us used to communicate in order to keep grown-ups' noses out of what we were doing. This time my letter was just a large question mark, signed M. I made an envelope with a sheet of paper from a writing pad, added a *calcomania* (transfer) for a stamp, and addressed it to The Raven. Then I put it through the gap at the bottom of her front door.

There was no reply to my letter. Carlota did not come to school the next day either. On the third day of her absence, two policemen climbed the stairs as quietly as they could. They entered Carlota's flat, where they remained for a long time. Worry was reflected in my mother's face. My sisters became more and more unsettled as the time went by.

I could not help thinking about Carmina. The vision of her dead in Don Cesar's arms brought fear, and my stomach churned. I had the dreadful thought that history would repeat itself.

I must have been in bed when the policemen went away, but gossip travelled from mouth to mouth. Senor Morales, the caretaker, told us the police had sealed the door. He also said that Carlota's parents were in hospital, seriously hurt.

As he disclosed the news, we learned that a gun battle between two enemy factions had taken place. Pistols and submachine guns sprayed bullets everywhere. Many people who were peacefully spending the morning in the park were wounded or dead.

I had never seen my mother in such a state of sorrow. Her praying habits had stopped with my father's illness. She no longer expected the mercy of the Lord to come to our rescue. We would have to rescue ourselves if we could. Senor Morales seemed to have come to the end of his story. He stopped a few moments, and then lowered his voice. He told us Carlota had died.

Desolation

Uncle Fabian often said that I had never been a child but was a grown-up in disguise. He chose opportune moments to tease me with this observation and would add: 'Your soul is not the soul of a child. Your body is just a disguise to confuse those around you.' His words, 'you have never been a child,' stuck in my mind and remained there to this very day when I am no longer nine years old.

I never protested. Neither did I give it a thought. But now that so many years have come and gone, I know that he was not completely wrong. I ceased to be a child early during the Civil War when the nightmare of killings started, when I did not know who the enemy was or where the next blow was going to come from.

After the funeral, I crawled up to Ali Baba's cave with a lump in my throat. It was cold, and our hideout had lost its warmth and enchantment. In the penumbra of that grey day, I could see the colourful book, *Arabian Nights*, lay on the floor. I stood with my back to the wall, looking at it until tears bathed my eyes and could no longer see. I remember picking up Carlota's cushion and hugging it to my chest. Then I found myself sliding down to the floor. The bullet hole became a tiny porthole into the sky, now dark.

I sat there immobile until exhaustion put me to sleep. And then I dreamt about Carlota, the Raven, and the adventurous times we enjoyed together. My dreams were only interrupted intermittently by the scenes in the cemetery: A white coffin taking my friend away forever; the lowering of that ominous box that contained her body into the grave; then the thud of soil hitting the coffin until it was completely covered.

I also dreamed of Uncle Fabian standing next to me with his arm around my shoulders, furtively in tears.

But in the cold reality of events, I caught a glimpse of him observing me not weeping; there was not a tear in my eyes. I could read his thoughts: 'Manolo was never a child. The war took that from him.' Maria, also by my side, held my hand in an abnormally tight grip that added to my agony, which I tried to suppress, as I had been told by my parents to do. I knew that the tears would come later when I was alone.

I do not know how long I was in Ali Baba's cave, shivering and sick with sadness, sleeping at times, dreaming, until a voice calling my name woke me.

'Manolo… Manolo, come, come with me.' I was too dazed to identify the nature of the call or who was calling my name.

'Manolo, come. You've been here all night. We thought you had gone with Uncle Fabian. Come home with me.'

Through half-closed eyes, I saw Maria's face. For a while I did not realize that I was trembling and that my sweater was wet with saliva and tears.

'Mum and Dad thought Uncle Fabian had taken you with him,' she repeated. Maria tried to get me up or at least to sit me, propping my back against the wall which had supported me before when my legs gave out.

'We must go home, Manolo, we must…'

I shook my head.

'Please!'

'I want to stay here – here with… Carlota.'

My final wish compelled Maria to stay with me.

Daylight was filtering through the gaps in the roof. The bullet hole became alive with the rays of the morning sun. My fingers were numb and my legs encrusted with the cemetery mud.

It had been raining copiously for several hours. Around the grave, soft mud, deep in places, was clear evidence that the heavens had opened. In this chilling and wet scene, I did not have to force myself to guess if my friend had been shrouded in the Raven attire, or even if the red scarf and black eye mask had been allowed to accompany her in the final journey.

People in black surrounded me. There were veiled women. Men's heads were uncovered. A scattering of policemen, friends of Carlota's dad, were there. A priest muttered something unintelligible and blessed the coffin as if that could bring my friend back. It was a useless effort that I sensed would do nothing for body or soul.

With Carlota's parents being critically injured in hospital, I wondered if it would have been better for them to have met with a quick death rather than survive without their daughter.

Maria consoled me with her presence and by talking now and then. Her voice not always audible. On reflection, she must not have known what to do other than stay with me.

One of our long silences was broken by Don Cesar's voice.

'Manolo, I think the pigeons would like to see you. They are waiting for their feed. Would you help me please?'

It was a clarion call to duty!

I composed myself as best I could. Maria dried my eyes.

'He must not know I've been crying,' I blurted out to her. It was a futile wish when my eyes were red and my limbs were purple with cold.

I crawled out through the entrance gap, following Maria, to find Don Cesar in a pretended attitude as if nothing had happened, which immediately gave way to a flood of tears.

I do not know how many days passed after Carlota's death, and even now I do not want to reopen the memories of those days when the first real blow of adversity hit me. Because of my stoic upbringing, I made the resolution to seal the remembrance of my friend well within my mind as if the tragedy had not occurred and consider what had happened as expected of the situation we were in. I did this in spite of feeling a permanent lump in my throat, and I went about my daily events with a heavy heart.

Very little was spoken about it between me, Juanito, and El Militino. One day after school, Juanito thought it a good idea to go to El Canalillo. So the three of us started on our way with our arms resting on each other's shoulders in a friendship chain. This time it was only three links, not four like when Carlota came with us. We walked in silence. There were no songs this time. Without her there, was no point to continuing. Suddenly, as if we were puppets on invisible strings, we unlinked our arms and silently turned on our heels back to our respective homes.

Sadness

In the Larrumbe School, there was a vacant place at the desk where Carlota used to sit. It was a vacuum that affected us all. I am sure Doña Amalia had to make a supreme effort not to say a prayer for the departed pupil and to avoid looking in the direction of the empty desk. My friends and I remained silent throughout. All our thoughts of mischief were gone. The chanting of the multiplication tables, capitals of the world, and other useful pieces of information were tarnished and sounded like a monotonous droning, not dissimilar to a late evening litany by the Augustinians.

One day, El Militino sat in Carlota's place. Juanito and I had also considered that, but it was El Militino's initiative that won. He remained there for a few moments and suddenly slid under the desk, accidentally upsetting the ink well onto his clothes. Maria Paz, who happened to be assisting her mother that day, came to help.

'What happened, Mili? Come up, please.' As she spoke, she bent over the desk to mop up the ink.

We could hear El Militino sobbing with a low kind of resignation that made some of us join in. When he came up from under the desk, his clothes were badly ink stained. His face was red and full of tears.

'That ink must be cleaned before it dries, otherwise it will never come out,' Maria said.

'My sister Amelia can do that, miss,' I told her. I really wanted to go home and away from class, and this was my opportunity.

'Go with Manolo, Mili.' Maria Paz shared our sorrow.

Amelia was happy to be useful. I was her pet, and so were my friends. With patience she worked on the ink stains, which were plenty, dabbing them with a cloth rag soaked in milk. El Militino parted with his pants and shirt while the cleaning was being done and a little while longer for them to dry.

My mother remained at my father's bedside, giving Amelia the chance of dealing with things on her own. Those were very sad and worrying days for the whole family, especially for my mother, whose tenacity for coping with the situation was crumbling.

A warm memory of my sister Amelia is always with me, especially now that so many decades have passed. And with the wisdom of age, I realize how much she must have suffered with an adverse psychological disadvantage and impaired hearing from of an attack of meningitis when she was little.

Going to school became a more and more painful routine, and remaining in class for the duration of the day was quite suffocating. Doña Amalia made an attempt to rearrange the position of the desks. That not only did not work but made things worse.

After class, my friends and I went straight to our respective homes exchanging only the occasional good-bye. After *la merienda* (five o'clock tea), we remained at home. Going to El Canalillo or even down to the street to play was out.

I did not see Juanito for a few days at school or anywhere else. Perhaps he was ill. Neither El Militino or myself had the strength to go and see him. After a few days of Juanito's absence, Doña Amalia had an announcement. Juanito's family had moved to another part of Madrid: Vallecas, I seem to remember. It was far enough to go and visit.

We were perplexed and explored all possibilities that our infantile minds could master. Perhaps the whole family had been taken for a stroll by the Reds and shot in some out-of-the-way field. Since this was often the norm, it became a favourite idea. I never knew how Juanito's father earned his money. Maria thought he worked in a bank and earned a lot, judging by the style in which their flat was decorated. It had heavy wood furniture and red and green linoleum on the floor, which was lavishly waxed. I saw a large case full of cigars there, and the dining room table sported a bowl with artificial fruits that attracted my attention. But whatever the reason behind his departure, we had lost Juanito. He was spirited away in a bizarre fashion.

Doña Amalia's announcement never rang true in my mind. Juanito and his family would just not move away without telling me or my mother, with whom they were also good friends. Also, Vallecas was no different than Outer Mongolia in our minds. My memory journeyed back to the evening when Juanito got hit by the stone in the eye. Then a flicker of suspicion, reinforced by my brothers' comments, led me to the truth. Now, after some weeks, having spoken to Rafael, it became clear that the activities of Juanito's father had been discovered and the whole family had been liquidated.

I never went back to help Don Cesar feed the pigeons. Passing by Ali Baba's cave was too much of an ordeal for me to endure. In my dreams, which reoccurred many nights, I was in the cave with Carlota, reading more of the wonderful stories in *Arabian Nights*, laughing, dressing up, and eating chocolate. But when morning came and I awoke, the dream dissolved on a pillow wet with tears. A heavy heart weighed me down for the rest of the day.

My father's condition worsened. He was on a road approaching a slow and painful death.

A telegram was sent to my brother Jesus He was with the army, either in Jabalcuz or Tembleque. I cannot be precise, but it was in the south of Spain. The telegram read: Dad critical. Come if you can. It was laconic but to the point.

There was no reply to the telegram. We worried again. We had not heard from him for a long time. Communication had been so far possible by letter, which could take an eternity to reach him. His reply subjected to similar delays. Besides letters, we got news about him in a more direct line when one of the soldiers who served in the same unit came to visit. This long silence unsettled my mother's mind more. Had he been killed in action? Had he been taken prisoner by the Nationals and put in a concentration camp? How would he survive there? I remember him at the age of nineteen when he was called up. In our minds, he had not been born to fight but to bring harmony to others.

When my emotional wounds had closed but not healed, I found out that Doña Marina had taken care of our cave, making sure that everything remained as it was the last time I was there. She regularly brought fresh flowers as in the hope that one day we could be together again. But her hopes were as impossible as my dreams.

The bullet hole in the ceiling remained there. It was an indelible reminder of the Raven. On reflection, I wonder how it never let the rain in. Was it due to the trajectory of the bullet or to some quirk of physics? Or was it just a tiny porthole to glimpse at the sky?

Often I wanted to have the courage to climb the stairs that led to Ali Baba's cave and stealthily squeeze through the secret gap to go inside, and sit on the cushion that Carlota embroidered for me, and feel the cosiness of our cocoon, and look at the sky through the tiny porthole, and see my friend smiling at me from beyond the clouds.

At times I found consolation in those thoughts. Then, reality hit me.

Death

February 22, 1939. My father died this day, and while he was dying, Pepe was in the kitchen throwing things about, amongst them a pot of soup that my mother had just cooked. On one side of the kitchen, there was a large, zinc washing basin with the dungarees he wore at work soaking in soapy water to dissolve the grease in which they were covered. In a rage, he threw the pot with the soup into it. All the time he was bawling and threatening my mother with a steel knife that he had fashioned at work. I am sure his intentions were far from killing, but only God knows why he was bent that way. He exploded into a rage whenever he felt like it, not for any known reason.

From where I was in my father's room, which was on the opposite side of the flat, I could hear threats and blasphemy. Pepe's behaviour should not be attributed to mental illness but to sheer and utter malevolence. I feel he must have been born like that, although that does not justify his conduct or the harm he inflicted in all of us.

My father was taking his final breaths. Saliva was regurgitating from his mouth when my mother joined us. She came into the room holding the thin kitchen-range poker that she grabbed to defend herself from my violent brother. She stood silently. Her eyes travelled from my father to the rest of us: Martina, Amelia, Maria, and I. Rafael was collecting timber debris for the range. Pepe was still in the other side of the flat, smashing whatever his hands could get hold of. Jesus was away; nobody knew where. Adelaida was in France, and Salvador was fighting for his life in a sanatorium. I could see despair in my mother's face.

Suddenly she blurted, 'You're leaving me with this lot… on my own.' It was an expression of total desolation.

My eldest brother was in a sanatorium, if you can call it that when it's a dilapidated building housing a few beds for people without hope. It is not easy to be given a bed there. You've got to know somebody who is "a somebody". My brother was in such a building with consumption. He was coughing and vomiting blood.

After my father's final gasp for life, we kissed his forehead. Then Maria and I were taken to Uncle Jesus's. I did not cry. I couldn't. Tears wouldn't come. I had seen so much death and human slaughter that my feelings were numb forever. I would know the truth of this when I grew up, when tragedy struck again, as it would. This is a fact that is imprinted in my mind. The enemy within is always alert to fend off happiness.

We stayed in a small room with Auntie Ignacia and Jesusin. Maria cried all the time, making me feel that was the right thing to do, and I wished my eyes could produce a flood of tears to join her. I forced myself to cry. It was a fruitless effort, which made me feel lonely and isolated. Somehow I had done all the crying I had to do.

Jesusin's eyes were bright with contained tears bathing the scorched corneas that looked less opaque than in previous days. But his vision had not returned. We hardly spoke. At the end of a prolonged silence, he fished his eyepiece from his pocket and started to draw another helmeted knight on horseback attired in colourful armour. Its shield and lance were at the ready. And there was an inscription:

Para Manolo. (For Manolo)

During the ensuing days, Maria and I went to Uncle Pedro and Aunt Dolores' for breakfast. They lived in Nuñez de Balboa next to our workshop and garage. Uncle Pedro seemed to us a surly man. But after getting to know him better, we realized he was kind and amiable. And so was Aunt Dolores. Breakfast was invariably *sopa de ajo* (garlic soup) with a poached egg floating in it. Afterwards, we drank milky coffee.

It's amazing what memories the brain retains. I remember a narrow bench of white wood with a metal latch that my uncle used for shoe repairs. I remember sitting astride that narrow bench after breakfast to rest before returning home.

Our cousins Paco and Pedro also lived there. The former was a turner operator in the workshop. Pedro's occupation was unknown except for the common knowledge amongst the family of his activity as a sniper.

One Last Week

I heard the war was about to end. So what! Peace is not going to bring back my childhood or reward me for the time spent in the mire. My mother and the rest of my brothers and sisters are alive; we are here in Madrid, waiting to be liberated. We've been waiting for this to happen since the war began three years ago. Madrid has ever since been in the clutches of the communist hordes that kill, torture, and maim citizens in the feared Russian style.

Towards the end of March, we had to endure the infamous week of the communists. A curfew was imposed well beyond the earliest reaches of my memory. It was a curfew that was not necessary, since nobody ventured in the streets after dark. Now there was something more horrible than that. Going out during the day was more dangerous than ever before. Diverse factions had taken to the streets, armed mainly with nine-millimetre calibre pistols.

Passersby, if any, were stopped at gun point, interrogated on the spot, and either shot or dismissed with a pat on the back. The spread of fear was without measure. We were constantly vigilant and trusted nobody. This was a civil war. The enemy was unknown.

We lived in a second-floor flat. Any sound of footsteps on the wooden stairs unleashed a nightmare of panic. Early one evening, in uncertain daylight, we heard the stairs creak. There were hurried footsteps. The trampling of soldiers boots came closer and closer to our landing. We knew that Madrid was about to fall. That had increased the policy of mayhem created by the Reds. Anybody could be snatched from their home on suspicion of favouring the "enemy" and taken to a ghetto for interrogation. Few returned.

Since my father died, I had been looking for the revolver that constantly accompanied him. It must have been somewhere in the flat, but I could't find it. Yesterday, somebody was shot dead in an upstairs flat. I was expecting something similar to happen to us. The Reds would knock the door down and take my older brothers or even my mother with them. If I could only find my father's revolver, I would not let that happen. I wondered if the trigger would be too hard for me to squeeze. Perhaps if Maria was with me, she could do that. She's a big girl, four years older than me.

The tramping boots stopped on the landing outside our door, followed by the thud of something heavy. My mother had gathered us all in the kitchen on the opposite end of the flat from the entrance door. She held the poker in her hand. Rafael got hold of an axe that he used to chop wood for the kitchen range. There was something bulging under Pepe's shirt. I could see the silvery butt of the revolver I couldn't find.

Strangely, I did not feel fear any more. None of us did. We had hardly existed. It had been a long time. What was it to us to live or die? We were expecting the door to be broken open. Instead, there was a knock, then another, and another. It was a knock that we recognised. It rang:

> Media copita de ojen
> Media de vino tambien.

We looked at one another with incredulous thoughts. The poker fell from my mother's hand. The axe was put to rest against a wall.

It was my brother Jesus on leave from the front line.

We all shared hugs and tears, then laughed at what did not happen.

He was on leave from the front line. How unusual! There was a reason: my brother's commanding officer detailed him to bring a food parcel to his wife and children in exchange for a week's leave.

We eagerly emptied his rucksack. There was a kilo tin of corned beef, a similar-weight can of sardines in tomato sauce, and two large loaves of bread. One was for us. The rest of the victuals were for the commanding officer's family.

Our famished bodies stood around this mirage. Manna from heaven that will last for a few days. And, all at once, we decided to appease our hunger, ignoring the consequences.

We ate the meat, the fish, and the bread with the kind of satisfaction that eluded us for long. But towards the end of my brother's leave, dark clouds set upon our family because he had to depart.

We thought of him receiving court martial, but that was futile! Those days, a bullet at close range was the solution for disobeying orders. Jesus had done just that by not returning on time.

My sister Martina had a pretty safe idea. She would walk to a military medical post not far from home and report Jesus sick. The chances of a doctor coming to check my brother's condition were nil. With no telephone or the possibility to send a telegram, that was the only way to pass along information. Martina returned home with a thumping heart. My brother's unit had been totally annihilated.

The Bitter End

It's April 1. The war was over. There was jubilation. People embraced in the streets. The shops were open without the fear of a hand grenade being lobbed into them. There was nothing much on sale, since the money that had been circulating during the past three years had no value now. Maria discovered that the stationers had penholders to sell, but no nibs. So, she bought two holders with a few coins she had.

El Militino and family have disappeared from the scene in a similar way as Juanito did. Nobody knows where they have gone.

Crowds gathered in the streets and walk down General Oraa towards La Castellana, a Madrid main artery where military parades take place. Martina, Maria, and I join them.

There was a mass of people waiting for something. The whole street was effervescent with humanity. In the conglomeration we lost Martina, obviously swallowed by the multitude. Maria and I stayed together, our hands glued to each other. We did not need to move or walk; the crowds took us like a torrential river.

I heard we were waiting for our liberator to drive past, the man who fought to restore the Spanish spirit that for centuries had been held together with the glue of Catholicism. A strident chorus shouted the Liberator's name. Everybody was delirious with joy. There were no more bullets, bombs, or destruction. A big man picked me up and put me on his shoulders so that I could see an open car surrounded by Moorish outriders on horseback and white turbans. It reminded me of the *Arabian Nights* and my lost friend. I shouted with the crowds until my throat ached.

Maria and I staggered home after hours with the grateful crowds. I lost a shoe while I moved with the multitude. I stayed at the entrance door to our block and looked down the street. None of my friends could come to join me. The ice-cold feeling of loneliness froze me to the spot.

The war was over. And now... what now?